The

Canary

An Owner's Guide To

A HAPPY HEALTHY PET

Howell Book House

IDG Books Worldwide, Inc.
An International Data Group Company
Foster City, CA • Chicago, IL • Indianapolis, IN • New York, NY

Howell Book House
IDG Books Worldwide, Inc.
An International Data Group Company
919 E. Hillsdale Boulevard
Suite 400
Foster City, CA 94404

For general information on IDG Books Worldwide's books in the U.S., please call our Consumer Customer Service department at 800-762-2974. For reseller information, including discounts and premium sales, please call our Reseller Customer Service department at 800-434-3422.

Library of Congress Cataloging-in-Publication Data
Grindol, Diane
The canary : an owner's guide to a happy healthy pet /
Diane Grindol.
p. cm.
Includes bibliographical references.

ISBN 1-58245-018-8

1. Canaries   I. Title
SF463.G75   1999   99-38338
636.6'8625—dc21   CIP

Manufactured in the United States of America
10 9 8 7 6 5 4 3 2

Series Director: Susanna Thomas
Book Design by Michele Laseau
Cover Design by Iris Jeromnimon
External Features Illustration by Laura Robbins
Photography: All photography by Eric Ilasenko
Production Team: Heather Pope, Linda Quigley, and Christina Van Camp

Contents

What
Is a

part one

Canary?

External Features of the Canary

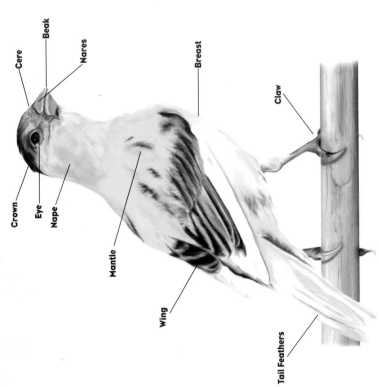

Cere

Beak

Nares

Crown

Eye

Nape

Mantle

Breast

Claw

Wing

Tail Feathers

chapter 1

What Is a Canary?

I casually mentioned to my mother-in-law one year that I had always wanted a canary. We were in a pet store, looking over a cage of the bright yellow birds. I admired their songs, so different from the sharp calls of the cockatiels I had at home. For Christmas that year I received one of the canaries we had been admiring, a yellow specimen with a few pleasing black markings. I decided to name him after a bird, "Martin" Luther.

Luther launched a whole new era in bird keeping for me. He was very different from the psittacine (parrot-like) birds I had been caring for over several years. He had different needs and behaved differently. His vocalizations were an attraction to me, as was his bright coloring and cheerful personality. He sang, bathed, sunned on the patio and lit up our life for many years. Though I could never suggest that you give a live animal as a gift, he represented the love of

The song of the canary can brighten any home.

my family and the care my mother-in-law took to give me exactly what I wanted that year for Christmas!

The song of a male canary brightens many hearts and homes. These colorful, active little birds may live ten to fifteen years. They readily eat fruit and vegetables or homemade treats, and male canaries grace a home with song for much of the year. Canaries will recognize

their caretakers or family members and develop certain personality characteristics. You may find that your canary loves music, for example. In fact, it may especially appreciate a certain kind of music. Many canaries will vocalize when they hear music that strikes their fancy. That may be classical, jazz, country and western or even opera. You have to hope that the two of you develop similar tastes in music. Canaries react to other household sounds as well. They may serenade you when the water is running or keep up with the din of a party at your home.

Canaries love to bathe and will appreciate fresh water in a special bath that clips onto their cage.

A friend of mine used her canary's penchant for bathing as entertainment for people who visited her house. Guests were treated to the whole show, and the canary was glad to oblige. Imagine visiting a home where the entertainment was not scintillating conver-

sation or the latest video but a bird taking a bath! Of course, the observers generally took a shower as well as the canary joyfully fluttered in its bathwater. Everyone had an enjoyable time.

What Is a Canary?

There are many breeds of canary, only some of which are yellow and only some of which sing well. There are canaries bred to have certain shapes, colors or feather qualities rather than for song. And there are canaries bred for song who look more like sparrows than Tweety Bird. There are even canaries who don't sing—in fact, most female canaries do not sing. The beginning canary owner might be totally amazed at how many shapes and colors canaries actually come in.

Where Do Canaries Come From?

The common canary, *Serinus canarius,* is related to finches native to the Canary Islands off the coast of Morocco. Originally, these islands were named after large dogs (*canis* in Latin) kept by local people in ancient times. So it is the dogs for which the Canary Islands were named, and the islands for which the canary birds were named. Europeans began making pets of the wild canaries, members of the *Fringillidae* finch family, in the fifteenth century. These finches are a grayish green color with only a hint of yellow on their breast, quite different from our modern canary. They actually look more like a sparrow than how we think a canary should look. The male's song was noticed and prized, however, and pairs were eventually kept in captivity and bred to enhance certain characteristics, such as song, feathering or conformation. Over the past 500 years, this has led to the development of numerous breeds of canary, all of which are vastly different from the original nondescript finch.

> ### BE DAZZLED AT A BIRD SHOW
>
> A good way to be able to compare the relative merits of the many breeds of canaries would be to go to a bird show. There are several in the country with a large number of canaries entered in the exhibition. It is truly an amazing sight to see many of the canary breeds in a single event. If you just want to see a singing yellow canary, well, there is probably one of those at a show, too!

This development of breeds is unusual in birds. We commonly think of dogs as being a certain breed, and sometimes they look very different, when you consider that a Chihuahua, Bulldog and Great Dane are all the same species. Most often with our companion birds, each different one is actually a different species, native to a different part of the world. Canaries are all

canaries, but they vary greatly in their looks and are
divided into several breeds.

Bred for Song or Type

The canary breeds break down roughly into those bred
for song, those bred for color and those bred for
appearance or conformation. The males of all the different canaries do sing, but the canaries bred for song
are real specialists in producing certain songs. They
are often highly trained, will sing on cue and need
to know certain notes to compete professionally.
Obviously, their owners are trained to hear these notes
as well.

*Canaries bred
for color can
come in daz-
zling hues, such
as this intensive
Red factor
canary.*

The canaries bred for color are conservatively shaped
but are available in colors that range from white to brilliant orange and many pastel shades of brown, gold
and silver. The list of canary colors is particularly lus-
cious. Don't you want to see an Isabel, a satinette, a
gold brown ino, a dimorphic, an intensive or nonintensive colored bird? The colors have technical names,
but in real life they look like a feathered rainbow. The
shades of red available in canaries derived originally
from crosses with the wild Black-hooded Red Sisken,
Carduelis cucullata, a native of Venezuela.

You may not recognize some type canaries as being
related to our favorite songsters. Type canaries are

bred for their shape and form. This ranges from squat to long, to tall and upright. There are type canaries with crests and those with frills and swirls of feathers that go every which way.

These fancy canaries often come in a variety of colors, making an even wider assortment of choices for the canary owner. One of your first decisions is whether to get a canary for its song or for its looks. Of course, you may find a bird with both attributes. I had the cutest

Some canaries are bred for looks, such as this crested Columbus fancy crest.

crested canary for a while. He was a soft yellow, with a perfect cap of dark feathers. I named him "Maestro," but he took his musical duties a little too seriously. Dear Maestro sang so loudly and lustily that I could not carry on a phone conversation in the same room with him. When I was approaching home, I could hear him outside from a few blocks away. My home at the time was small and busy with two dogs, other birds and a housemate. This was obviously not a good situation. I eventually found a home for him in a restaurant, where his loud singing rang cheerily over the din of conversation and clanking dishes.

Mixed Breed Pet Canaries

The different breeds of canaries are often bred by bird exhibitors and those who have developed a passionate interest in some facet of the canary keeping hobby. Often, pet canaries are bred with no regard for their backgrounds, genetics or lineage. These birds may be good singers but don't fit the description of any certain breed.

These are the "mutts" of the canary family. They come from a checkered background or are the family pet set up for breeding so their loving owners can produce another generation. You can't show a pet-quality canary of mixed heritage, but you can have a lovely companion all the same. Maybe you can find some of the characteristics in it that belong to the breeds!

My canary companion as I write this book, Skippy, isn't obviously any certain breed. He is a frosted apricot color, so I know that he has Red factor blood in him. He is a pet-quality canary; however,that doesn't lessen the enjoyment I get from his singing. Skippy especially enjoys the sound of water running and is a great companion when I do the dishes. Sometimes I even play him his favorite country and western music, even though it isn't my favorite!

Skippy delights in broccoli, too. I swear he could eat his weight in broccoli every day! This penchant for eating vegetables nixed any attraction to canaries for the teenage daughter of one of my friends. She liked everything about her canary, except that she had to feed him (yuck) broccoli or (yuck) spinach. How could he like that stuff?

A Canary Specialty: Sensitive Respiratory Systems

Canaries went to work with miners for decades because their extensive and sensitive respiratory systems meant they could detect lethal gases. Indeed, their respiratory system is one of the outstanding characteristics of canaries.

In birds and people, respiration supplies oxygen to cells in the body, with its main function to supply oxygen to the blood. Respiration also eliminates carbon dioxide and helps to regulate a bird's body temperature. A bird's method of breathing is unique and its respiratory system is complex, very different from our own. The system is not only complex, but lightweight, since most birds are built to fly.

We take a breath (breathe in and out) to circulate air through our own respiratory tract. Birds take two complete breaths to do the same thing. The air they breathe circulates not only through their lungs, but also through a set of air sacs. Air sacs are unique to birds and are located throughout their bodies. They lighten the body, another aspect of efficient, lightweight design in these flying machines, and they ventilate a bird's lungs.

Humans have a diaphragm that separates the abdominal cavity from the lungs. Birds do not have this apparatus, but use the keel bone to pump air in and out of the lungs. Bird handlers must take care not to compress a bird's chest; this would stop its ability to breathe.

In flight, a bird will fill its air sacs rather than its lungs with air, as this green Gloster consort is doing as it leaps from its perch.

In flight, wing strokes compress the rib cage and help a bird expel air. Like a bellows, the body wall of a bird expands and contracts with each breath. When a bird breathes, its body wall expands and fills the air sacs rather than the lungs. Birds breathe into their air sacs, then breathe out through their lungs and a network of bronchi and air capillaries where oxygen and carbon dioxide are exchanged. The role of the front air sacs is to take stale air from the lungs during inspiration and then expel it through the trachea during expiration.

THE UPPER RESPIRATORY TRACT

A canary's respiratory system is divided into two parts, the upper respiratory tract and the lower respiratory tract. The upper tract includes the nostrils (called nares), nasal and oral cavities, glottis and windpipe. There is a syrinx at the lower end of the trachea. This whole system cleans, moisturizes and warms inhaled air. The temperature can affect a bird's breathing. If a bird is chilled and its body temperature is lowered, its breathing slows to conserve body heat. When it's hot, a bird pumps fresh cool air through its system by breathing faster. Birds need more air than any other animal because of their high body temperature (105° to 112°F), fast metabolism and high activity level.

A bird's larynx is a passageway for air but does not produce sound as it does in mammals. That's our "voice box." In birds, the voice box is the syrinx, with a vibrating membrane at the end of the trachea, that produces sound through the vibration of airflow.

WHY CANARIES IN COAL MINES?

A canary takes about 60 to 100 breaths per minute. The rate can be quite variable, depending whether the canary is at rest, walking or in flight. A person's respiratory rate, in comparison, is sixteen breaths per minute. Your respiratory system takes up about 5 percent of your body volume. In a bird, the respiratory system takes up 20 percent or more of its body volume. Because of the surface area and volume of this system, birds are particularly susceptible to airborne disease and toxic fumes. Canaries taken into the coal mines would succumb to toxic fumes, alerting the coal miners to impending danger. Beware of fumes or smoke around your bird's sensitive respiratory system.

THE LOWER RESPIRATORY TRACT

The lower respiratory system consists of the bronchi, the avian air sac system and two small lungs with air sac membranes coating them. A bird's lungs exchange gases, oxygen and carbon dioxide more efficiently than those of any other animal.

Air Sacs

The avian air sacs add to the efficiency of respiration and help cool the bird. Half or more of air intake is used for cooling. Air sacs are found throughout the body and in the main bones, and a system of tubes supply fresh air through the lungs and bronchi to almost all parts of the body, including quills of the feathers. There are usually nine air sacs in a bird arranged in pairs throughout their body, with one unpaired lung air sac.

Your Canary Needs Air!

What all this means to you as a bird owner is that you will want to be careful about having your bird around fumes, chemicals or smoke, and be sure not to squeeze your pet canary, no matter how much you love it!

chapter 2

Canaries
Throughout
History

Having been in captivity for over 500 years, canaries have had a long relationship with man. Wild canaries are native to the Canary Islands off the coast of Africa, which are currently governed by Spain and Portugal. The export of wild canaries from their native habitat became a lively business in the sixteenth century, with bird catchers employed in the trade and sales contracts. The wild birds were bred first in Italy. Records show that Italian breeders were exporting canaries to Germany as early as 1622.

During the seventeenth century, canaries spread throughout western Europe and into Great Britain. In France, they became pets of the nobility, with ladies walking grandly about with gentle canaries perched on their fingers. There are accounts that, as early as the fifteenth century, the French aristocracy lined their bedrooms and

14

gardens with cages and aviaries. The keeping of canaries became a popular pastime, and by 1608 there were hundreds of birds being shipped to Marseilles, France, from the Canary Islands. A whole trade of "oiseliers," or bird merchants, existed.

Eventually the trade in wild birds ceased as breeders produced enough canaries to meet the demands of customers. In 1705, a detailed book on canary care and culture was published, listing at least twenty-seven different types of canaries. As it tends to happen when a wild animal is taken into captivity and domesticated, color variations began to appear in the birds. Stray white feathers appeared on some birds, whole white tails on others and the rarest of all was the completely clear yellow bird.

Canaries have been admired and kept as pets for over 500 years.

British Canaries

Canaries were being bred in England by 1675. In Britain, breeders began to develop birds with different shapes and plumage, which became the "type" canary breeds of today. Canary breeders in Britain enjoyed exhibiting their birds and formed national clubs that set rules and standards for showing birds. Some of the first rules for showing canaries were written between 1780 and 1790. By the time canary enthusiasts exhibited their birds at the national exposition at the Crystal Palace in the 1850s, there were several breeds in existence. These included the London Fancy, the Yorkshire, the Manchester Coppy, the Norwich and the Lizard. Many of the type canaries are named for the county in Great Britain where they were developed. British fanciers also experimented with crosses between their canaries and other species of birds such as linnets, goldfinches and Siskins. Most of these crosses were not fertile, and in canary culture they are called "mules." (A mule is an infertile cross between a donkey and a horse and engendered the use of this name.)

The height of canary keeping in England was at the end of the nineteenth century. Many working people kept canaries and earned extra income by breeding them. In the textile towns of Lancashire and Yorkshire, and in the Flemish district of London, there were many canary breeders. Usually breeders kept from fifteen to twenty birds in one birdroom and raised the chicks to sell. This was a pleasant way to earn a little money and have the cheerful singing of canaries about the house.

Color-fed canaries, such as this intensive Red factor canary, have been in existence for well over 100 years.

In 1871, a canary breeder noticed that feeding cayenne pepper to canaries during their molt produced a rich orange plumage. Of course it stirred up some debate in its time, but the practice of "color feeding" canaries continues to this day. You can still achieve soft color changes with cayenne pepper or paprika, or even by feeding carrots to your canary.

In Norwich, the English county for which another canary breed is named, the Norwich Plainhead and the Norwich Crested canaries were developed. In 1910, many part-time canary breeders, who usually were occupied in the boot trade for a living, shipped 30,000 birds a year. The Norwich City Soccer Club is popularly known as "the Canaries" even today. You can find information about them on the Internet at http://canary.fsn.net. References to the soccer team kept popping up when I was doing research for this book!

Canaries Go to Work

Coal miners in the Scottish Lowlands and in Yorkshire took canaries into the coal mines with them as early warning systems against combustible or poison gases. (The Scotch Fancy and the Yorkshire canary, both tall, thin breeds of canary, were developed in these areas. Another group of coal miners in Belgium developed a tall, slim canary of their own, the Belgian Fancy.) Birds are obviously smaller than people and gases affect them sooner. Even more importantly, their respiratory system is more extensive, with air sacs and hollow bones, making them susceptible to airborne gases and fumes. When a canary succumbed, it saved human lives (see sidebar on page 12 in chapter 1). This practice continued into the 1950s before the noble canaries were replaced with sensitive instruments.

Like their coal-mine cousins, modern canaries may become agitated or ill if exposed to fumes, and may give you an early warning of something dangerous in the air.

My own canary, dear Luther, on one occasion, let me know that a pilot light had gone out in the kitchen and was emitting natural gas when he started to bounce around his cage and chatter nervously. I appreciated the warning and took care of the situation.

Germans Develop Song Canaries

In seventeenth-century Germany, the region of Tirol, about forty miles west of Innsbruck, was a center of

*Hartz
Mountain
Rollers are
known for their
beautiful songs.*

canary breeding. Later, the villages of the Hartz
Mountains became important canary producers. By
1850, Hartz Mountain Roller canaries were being
exported to England and the United States. These
canaries were noted for their song rather than their
shape or color. At the end of the nineteenth century,
Germany was producing 800,000 canaries annually, of
which 300,000 went to America in groups of 10,000
each. Hartz canaries also found their way to South

America, other European coun-
tries, Australia and South Africa.
These were almost all male birds
exported as singing pets. A con-
tinuous, rolling song was favored,
and it was noticed that breeding
played a part in producing the
desired song.

Almost every German city had its
own canary club and held exposi-
tions during this time. The center
of it all, the village of St. Andreas-
berg, had twelve canary clubs, and most of the people
in town were involved in raising canaries in some way.

Canaries Serenade U.S. Enthusiasts

In America, the advent of regular steamship service
between Bremen and New York helped make canaries
popular. Between 1905 and 1915, 3,250,000 birds were
imported into the U.S., mostly from Germany.
Enterprising bird breeders started raising canaries
themselves, and clubs began forming in the United
States as well. In time, people banded together to form
national clubs, and bird shows became a popular fall
pastime for canary enthusiasts.

Birdman of Alcatraz

One of the more notorious canary fanciers in America
was Robert Stroud, a convicted murderer with a life
sentence. During his twenty years of imprisonment in

the Leavenworth, Kansas, prison, he was allowed to keep canaries. Eventually he had as many as 300 of them and was given two additional cells to hold them. With a good number of birds and time to make careful observations of them, he recorded symptoms of canary diseases and wrote two books on canary disease that were important in their time and are still read for their historical value today. Although they represent keen observation for an aviculturist of his era, modern bird medicine has progressed beyond Stroud's discoveries. Stroud marketed canaries and bird medications from his cell. It is reported that he sent letters to the outside world under canary cage papers.

A canary in a show cage awaits judging.

In 1942, Stroud was transferred to Alcatraz, the island prison located in San Francisco's bay. With a history of violent attacks on other prisoners, he was kept in isolation there and was not allowed to have his birds. Between 1952 and 1954 Stroud wrote the story of his life, which was subsequently made into a Hollywood movie *The Birdman of Alcatraz*, starring Burt Lancaster. Stroud died in 1963, never having seen the movie about his life because his Alcatraz warden would not allow it to be shown there.

Tweety

As a tribute to the popularity and ubiquitousness of the canary in America at that time, an endearing canary character came along in 1941. A man named Bob Clampett created a cartoon canary featured in the Avery/Clampett cartoon *The Cagey Canary*. Originally the bird was named Orson and was pink. The name Tweety appeared in credits for the 1944 *Birdy and the Beast*. Tweety's most famous line originated in a 1954 cartoon called *No Barking* in which he says, "I Tawt I Taw a Puddy Tat." Tweety is a canary-yellow, perpetual baby bird with a big head and a knack for staying out of trouble. He originated at a time when canaries were

the most common pet bird found in American house-
holds and is probably responsible for the popular per-
ception that canaries are vocal, canary-yellow birds.
There may well be a few canaries out there named after
the cartoon namesake, as well!

Popular Birds in the U.S.

It's easy to see how a charming yellow canary inspired the creation of the cartoon character Tweety.

For the most part, canaries were the only cage bird
widely available in the U.S. until the mid 1940s, when
budgies began to interest the public. In the 1960s, it
was the cockatiel that captured America's heart, and in
the 1970s, the lovebird. The 1980s was the decade of
the larger parrots. They were
imported in record numbers, and
breeders learned to successfully
hand-rear these birds.

Though not the only companion
bird available, the canary has
maintained its fans, and there are
still numerous clubs devoted to
the culture and exhibition of
canaries. Each fall, shows take
place throughout the country
featuring judging, public display,
sales booths and awards for the
finest representatives of respective breeds. There are
many song, type and color canaries in the U.S. and
plenty of pet-quality canaries that grace homes with
their song and chipper spirit.

20

chapter 3

Canary
Breeds

Song Canary Breeds

AMERICAN SINGER

The American Singer was developed in the U.S. by eight women who lived in the Boston area in the 1930s. The blueprint, or breeding instructions, for creating singers with a two-thirds Roller bloodline

and one-third Border canary bloodline was formally adopted in 1942. With this plan, you can create your own American Singer canaries in about five years, starting with the two other strains of canaries.

The American Singer has been a popular bird. This is a breed that was deliberately developed to have lots of variety in its song. Breeders crossed Roller canaries with Border canaries (a type breed) to

21

produce a pretty and free-singing canary. American Singers can be any color, including orange, though they must not be color-fed. Many of the prize-winning birds are green birds that look a lot like wild finches. They may also be variegated, with dark patches on a basically yellow bird.

The American Singer may sing some of the Roller tours (songs) or even Waterslagger notes, but overall should sing a variety of songs that are pleasant to listen to. When they are judged at a show, they must sing. Serious American Singer exhibitors separate their show prospects from the flock about two months before show season. The canaries are encouraged to listen to a variety of stimulating sounds, such as the song of a "tutor" (an older male canary with a pleasant song), recordings of other song birds or of classical music or the radio. Some breeders drape their prospects' show cages with sheets during the day. Several times during the day they remove the sheets. Usually a show canary catches on quickly and starts to sing shortly after the sheets are removed. In actual judging at a show, cages are covered with a sheet, and

The canary's song should be pretty and pleasant to listen to.

when they are uncovered, the canary has a chance to sing and be judged on its song. There's no guarantee how this will turn out, so the competitions can be exciting and challenging, and even surprising.

GERMAN ROLLER

This is an old breed of canary developed specifically for its quality of song. The German Roller canaries originated in the Hartz Mountains of Germany, particularly in St. Andreasberg. In the 1700s and 1800s, many working-class families raised and trained singing canaries for supplemental income. By the mid-1800s, canaries were making their way to the U.S. regularly. Between 1905 and 1915, over three million Roller canaries were brought from Germany to grace American homes, dispersed by German dealers in New York.

The German Roller sings softly with its beak closed. Its throat feathers rise as the bird sings a soft song that spans as many as three octaves, and you will often see them pictured this way.

Hartz Mountain German Roller (female).

Aesthetically, German Roller canaries are not striking. They have pleasant proportions and grow to 5½ inches in length. Their colors vary from yellow, white, green or gray to variegated canaries incorporating these colors. Occasionally Rollers are red-orange colored.

Roller canaries trained for exhibition learn the tours, or songs, this breed must know for song competitions. They may be tutored by their father, meaning they are allowed to hear his song during their own song development. Or they might be isolated from their father but allowed to hear the song of a masterful singing Roller. Another way to train a Roller in its chosen repertoire is to play a tape or CD for it that features an outstanding

Young canaries utter their first few notes at about 6 weeks of age.

example of the notes of the breed. If you wish to train and show these canaries to their highest potential, an interest in music is helpful and you probably should learn from an experienced Roller trainer.

In the early days of Roller canaries, when they were first being trained as songsters in the Hartz Mountains in Germany, young birds were exposed to talented songbirds, such as mockingbirds, for their song instruction. There was even a Roller organ developed to train young song canaries. The canaries who picked up song easily were kept for

breeding and the poorer performers were sold as pets.
After 200 years of excellent breeding, some quite good
songsters have developed.

Young canaries utter their first few notes at about 6
weeks of age. It takes them up to eighteen months to
develop complex song, which should be sung in a
rolling fashion. Roller canaries are bred to mimic
songs well, and good breeders realize that the lineage
of both the mother and father play a part in how talented a songster each chick will become.

*Young canaries
learn to sing
from a "tutor"
bird in competi-
tion song train-
ing cages.*

In their first few months of life, the young male
canaries are left in "flights," large aviaries that allow
flight, with their fathers. This is done so that the young
birds hear and hopefully learn the song of the older
males. By the end of October, most of the young birds
will have finished the molt, when they don't sing
much, and then will begin to sing lustily again.

Once they resume singing, the young males destined
to compete in shows are trained. They are placed in
individual cages that are enclosed on all sides but the
front. At first, the cages are placed side by side so the
birds can see each other and adjust to this situation.
Then partitions are put between each cage, and the
birds are moved to an isolated room with subdued
lighting. There are few distractions from singing
lessons in this quiet environment. Then a "tutor" bird

with an exceptional song is selected from the older males, and he is put in the room with his students. The goal is to train four of the young canaries to sing in unison so they can be entered as a team at song competitions. About three times a day, for up to a month, the lights are turned up for half an hour to encourage the young birds to sing the songs they have been listening to. Listening closely to their songs, owners try to select a compatible singing team. This training is, of course, for formal competition. Your training of a Roller canary as a pet need not be so rigorous. You may note, however, that exposing your canary to inspiring songs in its first year or two of life can influence the quality of its song.

GERMAN ROLLER TOURS (SOUNDS TO IDENTIFY):

- hollow roll
- bass
- water gluck
- gluck roll
- DBWT (Deep Bubbling Water Tour)
- schockel
- flute
- water roll
- bell roll
- bell tour
- hollow bell
- gluck

Occasionally a Waterslagger can open its beak in competitions to make louder notes, unlike the Roller, which cannot do so in competition without penalties

SPANISH TIMBRADO

Spanish Timbrados descend from Spanish birds that were bred with local songbirds. They have a loud, high-pitched song and can produce some clear, metallic tones and a chattering sound like castanets. Timbrados are green, yellow, white or cinnamon birds and are often variegated. They may have dark marks on their bodies.

25

WATERSLAGGER

The Waterslagger is a song canary that originated in Belgium and has a soft to medium-loud song. They are usually light yellow with some dark marks and can sing the Roller tours along with bubbling water notes of their own. Occasionally a Waterslagger can open its beak in competitions to make louder notes, unlike the Roller, which cannot do so in competition without penalties. They are a popular breed of canary in Europe and are becoming increasingly popular in the United States as well. True Waterslaggers can imitate the sound of a slow, babbling brook, and can speed up the song so that the water is "boiling."

A male variegated Waterslagger.

Type Canary Breeds

BORDER CANARY

The Border canary is a breed created during the nineteenth century in the towns bordering England and Scotland. These included the U.K. counties of Cumberland, Dumfries, Roxburgh and Selkirk. These counties each had their own local type canaries until 1882, when the Cumberland canary breeders and exhibitors decided to call their bird the "Cumberland Fancy." The Border canary breeders met in July 1890 and created a standard, calling their bird the Border Fancy Canary. Their club started with a membership of 643.

The Border is a typical looking canary, often yellow or light yellow. Although the original Border canaries were quite small, the modern Border standard calls for a bird that is 5½ inches long. It holds itself, ideally, at a 60° angle. Sometimes there is variegation on a Border canary, and the standard calls for those markings to appear as regular marks called "technical markings." A four-pointer has small ovals around each eye and three dark feathers toward the outer edge of each wing. A five-pointer has, in addition, dark feathers down the middle of its tail. Border canaries should *not* be color-fed to produce reddish birds.

A Gloster Corona (top) and a Gloster Consort (bottom).

GLOSTER CANARY

The Gloster Corona (or crested) canary is the bird with a hairstyle that makes it look like one of The Beatles. Ideally, Glosters have a circular cap of feathers that gives them quite a dashing appearance. Quite often this headdress is dark on a light bird, for a showy effect. Some Gloster canaries do not have a spiffy hairdo, and are known as Gloster Consorts.

Breeders pair crested birds with noncrested birds because breeding two crested birds to each other can be deadly to potential chicks. Glosters originated in the U.K. when a Mrs. Rogerson of Gloucestershire County crossed Rollers, crested canaries and Borders to create a new breed. They were first recognized in 1920 and have enjoyed a great popularity. The Gloster canaries are, ideally, no bigger than 4½ inches long. They are stocky birds, and the ones I have known are not only cute, but sing freely, making them desirable pets.

Norwich Canary

The Norwich canary is the teddy bear of the canary world. They are relatively large, heavy canaries that can reach 6 to 6½ inches in length. They were probably originally bred for their clear orange-yellow color. The Norwich has an impressive forehead, a thick neck and is full in the cheeks and chest and across the back. The orangish hue talked about in historical records may have originated from feeding the birds cayenne pepper before and during their annual molt. This is termed "color-feeding" and is still practiced for Norwich in the U.K. Instead of cayenne pepper, a synthetic red food is usually offered now.

Yorkshire Canary

If the Norwich is a teddy bear, the Yorkshire fancies itself a model. It is a tall, thin, long-legged canary. It was probably developed from the Lancashire Plainhead, the Belgium and the Norwich. Exhibitors started to exhibit a Yorkshire bird somewhere around 1860. The Yorkshire Canary Club was founded in 1894. The Yorkshire can be up to 6¾ inches in length, and stands tall so that its height is obvious. Yorkshires are available in many colors and can have variegations on them.

On the show circuit, Yorkshires that are all dark are called "self," and the term "foul" is used if a dark bird has light feathers either in its wing feathers or on its tail, but not in both. If there are light feathers in both the wings and tail, the bird is variegated.

Frilled Canary

There are several types of frilled canaries. They look like dust mops and are a challenge to breed to exacting standards for the amount and placement of frilled feathers. In the United States, it is most common to see the Dutch Frill and the Parisian Frill. Frilled birds have swirled feathers on the back, the chest and the flanks. Other areas of their body should be smooth on their large frames. The Dutch Frill measures up to 6¾inches long, and the Parisian Frill may be up to 8 inches long. Frills are considered difficult to breed. Other frilled varieties you may see mentioned are the Coloured Frill, Japanese Frill, French Frill, Gibber Italicus (described below), Giboso Espanol and Swiss Frill. There are also crested frilled canaries, the Florin and the Padovan.

LIZARD CANARY

Then there's the Lizard. We haven't suddenly changed subjects in this book; there are indeed canaries called Lizards. They are named for the scale-like look of their spangled feathers. Lizard canaries have neat rows of dark feathering over most of their body. If they were a cat, they'd be a tabby. They also have a striking cap of pale feathers on their head, making them quite interesting in appearance. This breed probably appeared as a mutation in France and was introduced to London by French refugees. The history isn't certain, but it is known that by 1846 there was a Lizard canary and a closely related "London Fancy" breed that no longer exists.

The Lizard is a spangled bird with either a gold or silver color and dark markings. These birds have no spangle before their first molt, and in later molts the desired pattern may become hazy, so there's only one show season when they can be entered in competitions. The Lizard has an area on its head with no markings referred to as a "cap." If this is not present, the bird is called a non-cap, but having a well-defined cap is preferable to Lizard breeders. The clear cap should extend from the top of the beak to the base of the skull, though, of course, there are Lizard canaries with more or less of this marking.

The Lizard also has a black, clear eyebrow defining the break between the cap and the eye. The beak and legs should be jet-black, and the bird should be generally stocky and have a broad chest and head. It is a small, active, attractive canary.

FIFE CANARY

The Fife canary is a miniature Border canary. It cannot exceed 4¼ inches in length, but in all other respects it is a Border canary. It is seen in several colors: yellow, white, cinnamon, silver fawn, blue, green, yellow and variegated.

The Fife is a smaller version of the Border canary.

Many Fife canaries are yellow variegated birds. This is a fairly recent canary breed that became popular in the U.S. in the early 1980s.

A Cinnamon Fife.

GIBBER ITALICUS

Technically one of the frilled canaries, the Gibber Italicus seems to have been created so that people know the meaning of the phrase "beauty is in the eye of the beholder." It is a lanky, thin canary with hunched shoulders and naked thighs. It has large eyes surrounded by naked areas and a flat skull. To many, this bird looks like a freak or a mistake. The Gibber Italicus is thinly feathered, but the feathers it does have are usually a deep canary-yellow. This breed may be up to 6 inches long. The Gibber Italicas was developed in central and northern Italy and was officially recognized as a breed in 1951. These birds have trouble balancing and often prop themselves up with their tails or hold onto cage bars for support. They eat a lot in comparison to other canary breeds, perhaps because of their scant feathering.

Color-Bred Canaries

No matter what color these canaries are, they are bred to show off their color as well as possible and to be excellent examples of it. The birds are up to 5½ inches long, including a 1⅜-inch tail. To show properly, they should stand at a 45° angle on the perch. Their head should be neither too broad nor too snake-like. For show, they are also required to have all twelve tail feathers and eighteen wing feathers.

The coloring of a canary may derive from its diet, as in this yellow Fife canary.

Color in canaries comes from a combination of their overall basic color, called ground color, and the black or brown pigment over the ground color. Of course, some birds only have a ground color and do not have dark pigment. The feather quality of the bird is referred to as frost or non-frost and affects how bright a bird's color appears.

GROUND COLOR CANARY

Canaries are basically either yellow, white or red. The yellow coloring of a canary comes from pigments deposited in its feathers, which it derives from its diet. If a canary is all yellow, it is known as clear. When it has a single dark spot it is ticked. When it has patches of dark and yellow, it is known as variegated.

Birds with light bands on the end of their wide feathers end up with softer colors and are called "frosts." Breeders usually try to breed frost bird to non-frost, which you may hear referred to as yellow and buff, intensive and nonintensive or hard feather and soft feather. All of these terms refer to the quality of feather— the long, skinny non-frost feather or the wider, light-tipped frost feather. These qualities give a canary an overall look of solid, bright coloring or lightly shaded coloring. There is also an ivory mutation that dilutes the color of a bird so that red birds turn rose and yellow birds are a lighter color.

A Red factor frost male.

DARK PIGMENTS

The two dark pigments, which may be superimposed over ground colors, result in different colored canaries. For example, black and brown pigment on white results in a bird called "optically blue." It isn't a pure blue like a budgie would be, but the effect of the layers of color look blue-gray to the eye. One of my favorite canaries was a blue bird named, quite originally, Blue. I bought him at a bird fair. One of the canary breeders there surprised me by telling me that he could produce white babies if I chose to breed him. To me, he looked very dark and the probability of a white offspring from this sparrow-like canary seemed remote. Obviously, though, the man knew I really had a bird with a white ground color covered with black and brown. Blue sang beautifully and turned out to be an attentive husband, which isn't necessarily the case with all canary couples. Blue did indeed sire white canary offspring!

When only brown pigment exists, the birds have red eyes as babies. Brown pigment on yellow ground is considered a cinnamon-colored bird. Brown pigment on a white ground results in a fawn bird. Black and brown pigment on a canary with a yellow ground color is called a green bird; black and brown on a red ground results in a bronze canary.

There are endless numbers of color mutations and patterns and combinations of both being bred. These include opal, agate, ino and satinette. A trip to a bird show featuring canaries and lengthy discussions with color-breeding breeders and judges will clarify canary coloring for you if it is of interest.

RED BIRDS

Canaries were successfully crossed with the Venezuelan Black-hooded Red Siskin in 1928 in Germany, the U.S. and England. This allowed canaries to develop deep red coloring that was not possible before the hybridization. It is likely to have introduced some element of wild song into canaries as well.

If you have an apricot, orange or red canary, it owes its coloring to a Siskin in its background at some time. These canaries have a genetic predisposition for acquiring red coloring from pigments. A yellow or white canary will not turn red if fed pigments during its molt but Red factor canaries can be fed coloring to increase their red hue.

Red factor canaries can be fed coloring to produce a more intense color, as in this Red factor male.

This is known as color-feeding and is discussed in chapter 6. If you choose not to color-feed a Red factor canary, it still may attain a brighter red coloring through feeding it foods high in carotene when it is going through its normal molt in the summer. Carrots are an example of this kind of food. Other common dietary sources of carotene include cayenne pepper and paprika.

The Red Siskin

This is a Venezuelan finch in which the male is a brilliant scarlet red with a black head and black wing markings. The male is quite attractive. The female is more subtly shaded. In our modern canaries, the Black-hooded Red Siskin *(Carduelis cucullatus)* heritage is apparent in rich red hues, but the Red Siskin is not often still bred with canaries. In its native country of Venezuela, it has always been a popular cage bird, though it has not been widely bred in captivity. This has become a cause for concern. There are only a handful of Red Siskins left in the wild. When it was found that introducing Red Siskin bloodlines into the canary gene pool produced the ability to attain the brilliant red and orange hues of Red factor canaries, extensive trapping for exportation occurred, seriously depleting the wild population. Many of the Red Siskins in captivity have been genetically intermingled with canaries, but Red Siskin enthusiasts have been trying to sort these captive Red Siskins out and once again breed them, and even explore the possibility of reintroducing some of the birds to their native habitat.

Dimorphic Canary

Another color-bred canary is the dimorphic. Its very name means that the males and females have different coloring. Males of this canary breed are usually light overall with points of color. Ideally, they have a mask of color on their face and flashes of deep color at their flanks, chest and rump. The females have less coloring. This color canary is also called a mosaic, and they are usually color-fed birds with red points on them. It is believed that the trait producing these colored areas, with a difference between males and females, was developed from hybridization in the past with the Red Siskin.

Show Classifications

At a bird show, the color-bred canaries will be divided into dark and light birds. Canaries are classified as melanin, if basically dark birds, or lipochrome if they are clear birds. Within each category, the birds are divided up by their yellow, white or red ground color.

Please Yourself

Ultimately, you should listen to and look at canaries and find one that will please you as a companion for several years to come. If you want a certain breed of canary, find out its life span from breeders, and ask if it is prone to feather lumps or other genetic problems. Regardless of the type you choose, your canary will make a wonderful companion. Enjoy!

Living
with a

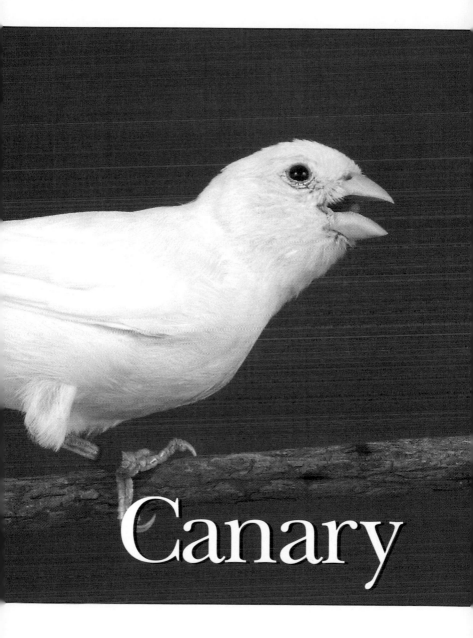

part two

Canary

chapter 4

Choosing a Canary

Canaries have much to offer. They do not require a great deal of handling because they are not social birds, like parrots. Instead, canaries are solitary, and your male canary will sing best if he is kept alone. Canaries are often acceptable pets in apartments, even if there is a "no pet" policy. It is rare that a neighbor complains about the song produced by a pet canary.

Canaries are easy on your nerves in our modern world with its busy lifestyle. Their gentle songs probably help us live longer, happier lives. Having a canary gives a person a reason to get up in the morning and something to care about! Canaries require relatively easy care and return affection by happily singing, begging for treats or maintaining eye contact with their owners. If you are interested in developing canary keeping into a hobby, it is very possible to breed and show canaries. There are bird shows held throughout the country in the fall. By attending a few, deciding on an interesting breed to acquire and learning more about breeding and showing canaries, you could start earning a few trophies and accolades from other canary enthusiasts.

Exhibiting in or attending shows adds travel and competition to the experience of bird ownership. It is also an excellent way to meet people who are as interested in their birds as you are in yours.

The joys of keeping a canary are both visual and aural. For most of the year a male canary will sing happily throughout the day. The summer molt is usually a silent, or at least a quieter time for canaries, but bursts of song brighten the rest of the year. In my household, singing is stimulated by water running or by playing a canary's favorite music. That music may vary for you and your canary. Some canaries favor classical, others pop tunes or country and western.

If you would like to train a song canary to sing the traditional songs of its breed, there are special recordings available from the national breed clubs. Rather than being genetically programmed to sing a species call, song canaries learn much of their song, and therefore must be "schooled" by a strong singer of their own species or by a recording of one. Of course, they'll learn some variation of whatever music you play, as well!

Aside from having canaries as pets, you may want to show your birds for fun and prizes. Showing will also allow you to meet other canary enthusiasts.

The music you provide at home is an influential part of your young canary's environment. Another influence is wild birds. Mockingbirds and starlings are great mimics in the wild and have complicated repertoires. Of course, song sparrows, robins and cardinals have their own special calls, and these may be something your bird adopts if it is exposed to them. If you listen for what your canary is hearing in your environment, a whole new world could open for you, one of wild birds, inspiring music and a keener awareness of your aural environment.

Selecting a Canary

A major choice for you when selecting a canary will be to decide if you prefer a type canary, a color canary or a song canary. If you are not concerned with your canary's appearance or abilities, you should be able to find a pet-quality canary of no specific breed. Any male canary will sing. If you get a song breed, you have an idea of how the bird will sound. For the others, if song appeals to you, you should probably listen to the song you are getting before acquiring the canary. Stand quietly near a cage of prospective canaries and listen. You may have to come back several times, or you may be lucky and find the perfect canary in one try.

Remember that if you are looking for a songbird for your home, you will want to select a single male as a pet. Females only rarely sing, and if they do sing, their song is usually soft and muted. Canaries are also independent birds. A canary will sing more strongly alone than if you keep more than one canary. It doesn't need bird company, though it will appreciate your attention and will enjoy watching other kinds of companion birds if you have them.

BUYING A PEDIGREED CANARY

If you choose to get a canary of a specific breed, you will probably want to shop for it at a bird show, or through ads at a bird club, a national magazine or an Internet list, or a national specialty society. Here are some suggestions of breeds that are commonly available and that would make good pet canaries:

Song Canaries

American Singer Canary

Roller Canary

Waterslagger Canary

Timbrado Canary

Type Canaries

Fife Canary

Border Canary

Gloster Canary

Lizard Canary

Color-Bred Canaries

Dimorphic Canary

Red factor Canary

Personally, I keep a canary as a "pet" for my parrot and cockatiels. The birds have each other for company, with the quick actions of the canary entertaining my psittacines (parrots). My canary watches the other birds, often eats when they do and entertains us all with cheerful song.

Hand-Fed Canaries

You might be lucky enough to find a canary that has been hand-fed from a breeder or pet store. Canaries are not regularly hand-fed as many of the parrot species are. For one, they are very tiny as babies and require frequent feedings that are too demanding for the schedules of most people. Canaries are also not intended to be hands-on pets, so socializing them at a young age isn't particularly important. When a breeder saves a chick from parents who have passed on or who aren't caring for it and hand-feeds it, the hand-fed chick often flies after its adoptive "parent" and learns to perch on them willingly. You might be able to find a hand-fed chick, but if not, you'll still enjoy your new canary.

A bird show might be a good place to find a special canary, like this variegated male Gloster Corona.

Where to Find Canaries

Most canary breeds have national specialty societies, and some bird clubs have members who are also specialty club members. Another place to look is in the canary classified ads in national magazines. You will find bird enthusiasts and canaries themselves at fall bird shows. These sources should lead you to a breeder who has the kind of canary you seek. If at all possible, get references or a recommendation of a breeder to buy from. You will want to be treated fairly and will want to receive the kind and quality of bird you are looking for. Recommendations can come from an avian veterinarian, a satisfied customer or someone who is actively involved with the type of canary you seek. At bird shows, you will usually find breeders of the many breeds who work hard to produce birds who meet the breed standard and will win at shows. They should be willing to sell you a pet-quality bird from their stock, or help you get started in developing your own stable of show birds.

I bought a cinnamon canary at one such show. The gentleman who sold it to me explained a great deal about canary care and expressed an obvious love for his birds. When the bird I purchased turned out to be a hen instead of a male singer, he wrote to me and offered to trade her back. This bird paired up with my blue male and they made such a happy couple I wouldn't think of returning her, but I appreciated his professional attitude and willingness to make things right.

When I wanted a Gloster Corona canary, a bird show was exactly the place to obtain one. Our local stores and the feed store often had canaries, but usually they were Rollers or Red factor canaries. At a local show, however, I had a wide selection of Glosters to choose from. "Maestro" delighted me with his mop of "hair," just like the pictures!

THE ANNUAL NATIONAL CAGE BIRD SHOW

One of the places to see the best canaries in the country, and to meet canary breeders, is the annual National Cage Bird Show, which has been held in a different city each year since 1949. You will be amazed at the number and kinds of canaries! Consider joining their organization, or look for their annual show date on the internet or in bird magazines. Find out more by writing:

NATIONAL CAGE
BIRD SHOW CLUB
25 Janss Rd.
Thousand Oaks, CA 91360

Canary Bands

You may see that many of the canaries you look at have bands on one or on both of their legs. Bird breeders often put an identification band on a canary chick when it is still in the nest. As the bird's foot grows, the band can no longer be removed and serves as permanent identification. Usually the band has a code on it for a national or local canary society, a code for the breeder and an identifying number for that band alone. It becomes a good resource for the breeder who is tracking the genetics of his birds. Bands are color-coded by year, so you know how old a bird is when you buy it.

Breeders are also interested in which of their chicks are males or females. Sometimes they put plastic "family" bands on the birds to mark whether they are male or female (red for female, blue for male), and another plastic band to identify the pair the bird is from. These family bands may be any color. The plastic bands can be applied or removed at any time; they aren't closed bands for permanent identification.

Bands serve as identification, but they are not "tags" required by state or local governments the way dog tags are. They don't show that a health vaccine has been administered and don't tell you who a bird's owner is. If you've been a dog or cat owner, this might be a new concept for you!

Leg bands, like the blue one shown here, are used to identify various details about a particular bird, such as age, sex, family and breeder.

Bands are usually helpful identification but can be dangerous if there are loose wires sticking from your cage or aviary A bird can get caught on a wire and injure its leg or worse. Every few months take a good look at your bird's accommodations and make sure they are safe.

Also observe your bird closely whenever you service its cage and give it food. One of the things to watch for is swelling under a band. If the bird worries at the band or has a leg problem that causes swelling, you will want to have the band removed by a professional. Do not, under any circumstances, try to remove the band yourself. You may break the bird's leg or otherwise injure it. Your veterinarian has special tools designed to remove bands. Many people then make up a record card listing the bird, its breeder and other information and attach the cut band to it.

It's That Time of Year . . .

Timing may be important in the success of locating the particular pet canary that you want. It is advisable to shop for a canary in the fall, when breeders are choosing their breeding stock for the next year and selling the year's chicks. Male canaries are singing in the fall, even those just hatched in the spring, so you can hear the song of the bird you are acquiring.

There are traditional times of the year to breed canaries. It's traditional for breeders to set up their birds on February 14 (time for romance!), and of course it takes a while for the birds to settle down, build nests, lay eggs and raise their young. Male canary chicks do not give a hint of their sex by singing their first notes until they are around 10 weeks old. By this time, the summer is starting to roll around. June through September is usually when canaries molt. Most molting canaries do not sing, so you can't hear what your new pet will sound like. If you want a canary who sings a pleasant song, you really do need to hear it first. Breeders are busy providing molting birds with extra treats that provide the energy they need to grow new feathers. By the fall, breeders can see and hear the quality of the youngsters they have raised, and choose the best for the fall shows and for breeding the next year. They will also be looking for homes for the canaries they cannot or will not keep, and by the fall a breeder is pretty sure which of the canary chicks are males or females.

Buying a Canary from a Bird Breeder

The main things to look for in a canary are that it comes from a clean environment and it is a healthy bird. The breeder you buy a canary from should be willing to provide you with a guarantee of health. He or she should also be willing to answer your questions and to provide you with information about the clubs, societies and shows where you can find out more about the type of canary you are purchasing.

Customer support is important to you as a new owner. Some of the breeds are prone to particular problems. The breeder should be open with you about that, and how he or she deals with the problems. The color-bred canaries may need to be color-fed to maintain the color you are looking at in your new bird. If your bright red bird turns out to be yellow next summer, you may not be happy! You should discuss diet with the breeder. It's best to keep a new bird on the same diet it's on when you first get it. What is the bird's diet, where can this food be purchased, what supplements does the breeder use? You'll also want to know what the canary likes to bathe in. The more information you can get from the breeder about your new bird, the happier you will be with your purchase. Birds are most comfortable with what they know. As your canary makes a transition from its former home to yours, providing it with familiar things will help it settle in. These include its food, feed dishes, bathing dish, cage size and a schedule that matches the breeder's schedule.

Gift Canaries

Living animals do not make good gifts, and they especially don't make good "surprise" gifts. The choice of an animal involves a person's commitment to that animal's welfare and upkeep. It is also a very personal decision. Both animals and people have distinct personalities and personal preferences. Sometimes the "chemistry" is there and sometimes it isn't. Also, canaries come in many different colors, which most gift recipients would probably rather choose themselves.

Beware of giving a live bird as a gift—make sure the recipient truly wants a canary, or let them choose one themselves.

45

Even more important, canaries are usually kept for their song. You will please your gift recipient the most if he or she can choose a canary with a song that person finds pleasing. After all, there are soft and loud songs, fast and slower songs, twitters and choppy beats to name a few.

If you know you want to give someone a canary as a gift, there are many ways of approaching the gift-giving without actually presenting a living bird. For example, you could get a gift certificate from a breeder or pet store that has canaries. You may offer someone a good book about canaries (what a great idea!) along with some of the initial supplies they would need and then offer to go with them to pick out a companion canary. You could get a canary tape and wrap it up in a nice size cage for this special person. You could wrap a breeder's phone number or a photo of a canary in a box, in a bigger box, in a huge box, making gift-giving a sort of treasure hunt. You could offer to go to a bird show with the gift recipient and buy him or her a canary there if there's a breed or an individual canary that strikes his or her fancy. Your options are many and various. It just isn't a good idea to pick out a live canary and present it as a gift. If you just acquired your canary, then you're probably reading this book to learn more about your new pet. Congratulations! Have many a melodious memory over the years with your new friend.

> **QUALITIES OF A
> HEALTHY CANARY**
>
> Clear, bright eyes.
>
> No evidence of nasal discharge; no wet feathers above the nostrils.
>
> Clean bottom; vent is not messy.
>
> Active and lively.
>
> Sings (if a male).
>
> Does not wheeze or gasp for air.
>
> Legs are smooth and shiny, not rough or lumpy.
>
> Stands up well, is sleek and smooth, not puffed up or supporting itself against the perch or side of the cage.
>
> Stands still, without pumping its tail.

Looking for a Pet-Quality Canary

When looking for a pet-quality canary, the supply will be biggest in the fall, but you can find them many times of the year. Places to look for pet-quality canaries include pet stores, bird clubs, bird fairs or marts, feed stores and local breeders. These breeders may produce canaries for fun or extra income but not for exhibition or to breed to a standard, like those who specialize in the breeds of canary. They would match up birds they like and create good "pet-quality" canaries, which probably come in many colors and have some quality of song. You can find local breeders by asking an avian veterinarian for a referral, or by asking a satisfied canary owner. There may be bulletin boards up at feed stores and pet stores with bird breeder cards. It is very possible that your area bird club can refer you to a canary breeder as well.

If you decide to purchase a canary at a store or from a breeder, your main concern should be to obtain a healthy canary. This is most likely if the environment in which the bird is kept is clean. Bird cages should be cleaned daily, and both food and water should be offered daily if not more often. Does the cage floor show signs of daily cleaning or sweeping? Is the staff knowledgeable and helpful? You may very well have some questions about canary care in the first few weeks, and it's nice to know where to get answers. Look closely at prospective canaries and observe if they are active, singing and look healthy. Can you get a guarantee that the canary you purchase is a male? If you are looking for a singing canary, that is important.

When purchasing a canary from a store or breeder, make sure the facility is clean and that the birds are being treated properly.

If you are looking for a songster, it is advisable to stand quietly at a cage and listen until the bird you are interested in actually sings. Is it pleasing to you? Can you listen to that song often, carry on a conversation over it and be happy doing housework to that song? Your pleasure in your bird's song is the ultimate quality you are seeking in a song canary.

*Listening to a
singing canary
before you pur-
chase it can
help you find
the bird you are
looking for.*

Both stores and breeders should be willing to offer a health guarantee for your new canary, giving you time to take the canary to an avian veterinarian. Though you have looked your new pet over thoroughly, avian veterinarians can perform a closer inspection and are aware of the subtle signs of common canary maladies. They can also do lab tests to tell you more about the health of your canary. Most bird illnesses are not visible to the eye but will be apparent in a bird's blood and

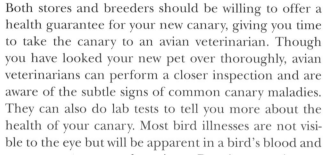

droppings. Parasites, respiratory infection, viral infection and feather lumps are concerns for new pet owners. An experienced avian veterinarian will know how to diagnose and treat these conditions.

Canary Care

Canaries are living beings and deserve daily care. Be sure that you have time in your schedule, or can arrange for help, to clean the cage daily and supply your canary with fresh food and water. It is important to know what foods you can give your canary so that it sings its best, molts annually with no difficulty and maintains its good health. Likewise, providing a good environment for your bird will keep it happy and healthy. You may wish to take advantage of various conveniences (discussed below) that help maintain cleanliness and a stable environment.

To contain seed or feed and flying feathers, you could consider a cage skirt, or a plastic mat of some kind under your bird cage. Some larger cages come with seed/feed guards on the cage or extending out from the bottom. There are also cage covers available that help you ensure that your canary gets a good night's sleep. A cage cover should be dark-colored, heavy cloth so your canary truly gets its rest in the dark.

For light, you may be interested in supplying your canary with some daily time under full-spectrum lighting. This helps a bird assimilate vitamin D_3 and calcium, and is a pleasing light that really shows off a bird's natural coloring. You can put a full-spectrum light on a timer so that your canary receives a consistent schedule of light and darkness. Sunlight is natural "full-spectrum" light, but as it passes through a window, the filtered rays lose some of their beneficial qualities. Thus, some artificial full-spectrum lighting is good for birds.

With any bird, a broom or a vacuum is essential to control the feed, feathers and dust generated by your pet. The choice is up to you. Just use it often! For spot cleanup, often a small vacuum is useful. Remember to do any cleaning with natural ingredients instead of with products that contain strong chemicals or produce noxious fumes. You can rediscover the benefits of cleaning with vinegar, lemon, baking soda and bleach (in a ventilated area) through bird ownership. There are books available on making cleaning solutions with these and other safe ingredients.

Daily food and water changes, as well as routine cage cleaning, will keep you and your canary happy.

There are numerous kinds of feed and water dispensers on the market. Some ingenious feeders keep the food in the middle of the cage, and that helps keep the mess inside the cage. Many water containers can be accessed from outside the cage, another time-saver. There are also various clips that allow you to clip greens, millet spray or cuttlebone to your canary's cage. You'll find this a fast way to offer treats.

Why Choose a Canary?

There have been times in American history when it was most likely a bird owner would have a pet canary. Now, there are a variety of pet bird species available. So, what makes a canary an enduring choice for many people, and why is it a better choice than ever before for the modern lifestyle?

Canaries, with their beautiful song and vibrant color, can really make a house feel like a home. They are small birds, so that their living quarters and supplies fit into small homes or apartments. With so many people on the go, busy with their jobs and lives, canaries are accommodating pets that do not need a great deal of attention to be happy. Canaries are generally truly caged birds, as well. They live in their cage and do not come out to soil their owners' living spaces or to destroy their valuables.

Providing your canary with natural, unfiltered sunlight is beneficial, but make sure it has a shady spot to retreat to if it gets too hot.

Most often, canaries are acceptable pets who do not make "noise" that bothers neighbors. If anything, your neighbors will enjoy a canary's beautiful singing as much as you do. They are gentle animals who delight in their lives and enhance yours. A canary will give back the love, care and attention it receives in numerous ways. It will chirp happily to see you, wait expectantly for its bath or eagerly anticipate its breakfast. It will acknowledge your taste in music, or sing along to its own favorite pieces.

A canary provides all this and more to people of many ages and walks of life. Busy professionals can have a pet to greet them after a day at the office, but don't need to rush home to look after it. Families can have a cheerful occupant who teaches responsibility and graces the home with a minimum of care. Older folks can find in a canary a companion, a responsibility or a new hobby.

Many retired people start breeding birds for exhibition or a small income. Teenagers who learn to care for and raise canaries, or any bird, learn about responsibility, sales and life (including death). For urban farmers, 4-H offers units on bird breeding and care. Canaries make delightful companions for single people, families, the young and the old.

Canaries and Children

Children can grow up with delightful song in their lives when a canary lives in their environment. Through helping provide its needs, seeing yearly changes a canary goes through and even watching a breeding pair raise young, children learn respect for life.

Very young children usually cannot care for a bird on their own; they need support from an adult who will help them remember about daily care and who takes on the responsibility of providing what a young child forgets. Older children who show an interest in animals may delight in having a canary or helping to care for the family's canary. Children exposed to a companion canary may start to become curious enough about birds to watch wild birds, provide wild birds with food or start on a career path in biology, zoology, ecology or animal medicine. At the least, they may continue to have companion birds in their lives, or could eventually participate in the fulfilling and enriching hobby of exhibiting birds.

Canaries in Public Facilities

A woman in San Jose, California, has provided hen canaries to both schools and senior centers in her area. Older hens are no longer useful to breeders but are perfect for classrooms because they are quiet. Occasionally, canaries come her way through the local humane society or from bird club members when they change lifestyles or when a canary breeder passes on.

Living with
a Canary

In senior centers, canaries liven up what can be a sterile environment and provide entertainment for the center occupants to watch. Seniors bring treats to birds, learn their names and talk to birds, which is good for all concerned! For someone who takes on this public service, it is a good feeling to connect birds who need homes with people who can appreciate them. For more information, please contact Sharon Scotti at (408) 255-5247.

An aviary can be a delightful addition to a restaurant, hotel, mall or other public area. People get a lot of joy watching and listening to birds in an aviary, usually stopping to talk to them or marveling at the colors of their feathers. Canaries can learn to be social enough to commune with visitors, as well!

WHERE TO FIND A PET SITTER

National Association of Professional Pet Sitters
1200 G St., NW
Suite 760
Washington, DC 20005
Referrals to pet sitters:
(800) 296-PETS
Phone: (202) 393-3317;
fax: (202) 393-0336
http://www.petsitters.org

Pet Sitters International
(offers referrals to pet sitters nationwide)
(800) 268-7487

Pet Sitters International
418 East King St.
King, NC 27021
(910) 983-9222
http://www.petsit.com/

Pet Sitters

Another responsibility of pet ownership is providing for your canary when you are on vacation. When you are gone on vacation, you should be willing to arrange for a friend, relative or pet sitter to come to your home to care for your canary. An alternative is to take the canary, its cage and supplies to stay with a friend or relative. Many veterinary offices and pet stores will also board birds. Some kennels accept birds. If a kennel in your area boards birds, be sure the birds are in a separate room from dogs and cats. Being exposed to these animals could be very stressful for your pet, and your canary should not be near the strong disinfectants and chemical products used around the dogs and cats. Whoever takes care of your pet bird should have some experience with birds. It's a little known fact that many of the major theme parks have animal boarding facilities on-site. Just because you have a pet bird with you doesn't mean you have to pass right by Disneyland if that's on your route. Call ahead or check the appropriate Web page to find out if your next destination can accommodate your little friend.

Hiring a pet sitter to care for your bird in its own home is a natural way to provide the least stressful care for your pet while you are away. Two national pet sitting organizations have referrals to their members throughout the country (see sidebar on previous page).

When you leave your canary with a sitter, make sure you leave detailed instructions, as well as the phone number of your bird's veterinarian and where you can be reached.

When you leave an animal with a pet sitter, assume he or she knows nothing about canary care. Provide a detailed list of instructions. Show a pet sitter where you keep supplies, from cage lining paper to seeds and fresh vegetables. Leave a pet sitter with vital information such as where you will be, who your veterinarian is, and contact information of friends or family who are familiar with your birds if something goes wrong. You should probably inform your veterinarian that you are gone and that your bird is in the care of a pet sitter, or provide your pet sitter with a form stating that he or she has your permission to take your bird to a veterinarian if it needs care. You can also ask a pet sitter to bring in the mail and the newspaper, water plants and change lighting in the house, providing you with theft-prevention services as well as pet care.

chapter 5

Caring

for Your

Canary

Bringing Your Canary Home

Once you've chosen a canary, you will be excited about bringing it home and setting up a place for it in your living quarters. How should you welcome your new canary and what kind of accommodations should you set up for it? To start with, how are you going to get it home? There are any number of travel carriers that you can use to pick up your canary. A temporary carrier can be fashioned from a cardboard box with holes punched in it.

You actually want a fairly small carrier so the bird isn't flying frantically into the walls. It can be made of wood and wire, Lucite or plastic. Be sure footing is not slippery by providing a paper towel or a terry towel in the bottom of the box. If you're creative, you can position a branch or dowel perch in the carrier not far off the floor.

You could use a small cage as a carrier, being sure not to have water in it and to remove any swings or toys that might hurt a bird by swinging about wildly. Instead of water, provide orange slices, apple or greens to your canary while traveling. Those don't spill but provide moisture if the bird needs it.

I think every bird owner should have a carrier on hand for an emergency situation. Maybe you should be prepared and get an airline kennel so you are ready if you and your canary ever fly off on a trip together. Both pet stores and airlines sell "airline kennels." You might want to set up a perch in it for your bird.

Birds are sensitive to temperature changes. If it is relatively cold or windy when you pick up your canary, use a towel to wrap its cage. Then take it directly from a heated store or home to its cage. In the summer heat, your canary will need to be kept cool. Of course, you can use an air conditioner in your car. You may also spray the bird with water if it starts panting and holding its wings out to its sides. Those are signs of overheating in a bird and require immediate attention. Remember not to leave your bird in a hot car; if you need to do other shopping, do it before you buy your bird.

Shipping Canaries

If you are having a bird shipped to you, you should be aware that airlines will not ship birds when the weather is excessively hot or cold. Most people use a counter-to-counter service to ship animals with great success. Check with an airline for more details. You will need an airline kennel, with sloping sides and adequate ventilation, for shipping a bird. Also check with your avian veterinarian about state requirements for a health certificate. It is possible to ship small birds, like canaries, via the post office. Of course, you can't do this over a holiday or even over the weekend. Talk to your local post office or access USPS (United States Postal Service) information on the Internet to find out more.

Quarantine

If you have other birds at home, it is important to quarantine any new birds you bring into the house. This is an initial period when you keep the new bird separate from any other birds in your household. Though a separate building would be ideal for this, most people

During the quarantine period, do not handle your new bird before you handle your other birds without washing up first.

quarantine new birds in a bedroom or a bathroom. During this time, you will be watching the new bird for signs of illness and should take it to an avian veterinarian for a "well-bird" check.

Treat this new bird as though it has a disease that could be transmitted to the rest of your flock. You can do this by being careful during your routine care. Take care of your new bird last. Don't handle your new canary, then handle your other birds, without first washing up. Don't dip the quarantined bird's bowls into a communal feed supply. You should have a separate feed container for this bird, or at least have a scoop in the feed container you can use to fill up feed bowls. If you can, wear a separate smock in the new bird's area, and take off your shoes or change socks before entering its area. Quarantine should last from a month to forty-five days, after which time the new canary can join the flock.

Setting Up an Environment

A new canary needs some supplies, and you require some to help care for it. You'll be creating an environment for your canary in your home, and want to make it happy as well as keep it healthy. Ask yourself the following questions when choosing bird cages and all of your bird accessories: Do you like the looks of what you're buying? Does it clean easily? Is it good for your

bird?

The Cage

Canaries are usually kept in cages as pets. Their accommodations may range from outside aviaries to inside flights to an alcove in your home. Canaries can also have a cage they call home but be allowed free flight in a home. Canaries with free flight can learn to return to their cage after getting their exercise. I have also known of canaries who had the use of a whole porch, with branches and ropes and perches supplied for their use. Use your imagination!

You will need to be able to keep a canary's environment clean and to have easy access to its food and water. A cage or aviary should also be safe from predators. These range from a household cat or dog to wild animals outside.

For your caged canary, choose a cage that is attractive to you but also easy to care for. Cutting circles out of cage liner is not fun, and you will tire of it fast. Choose a rectangular cage. A cage at least 24 inches long is best and actually gives your canary some room to flit lengthwise quite some distance. A 36-inch space would be even better!

Another consideration is the size of your daily newspaper, the popular choice for lining cage bottoms. The best size cage is one in which your newspaper fits perfectly. If it weren't for changing the papers in the bottom of the cage, I wouldn't get caught up on a lot of the news around our town.

The bar spacing in a cage should be close together, made especially for canaries and finches. If bar spacing is too wide, then a canary could fly through or could get its head stuck between bars. It's not a good idea to have decorative scrollwork on a cage. A canary might catch its band, a wing, head or a foot in the odd spaces created by such decoration. Safety first!

You will have the easiest time caring for the cage if food and water dishes are accessible from outside the cage or aviary. A nice extra for active canaries is a seed guard on the side of a cage.

Color is up to you. There are a wide range of colors and finishes available, ranging from metallic to bright, modern colors.

If you opt for a used cage, check for rust. Rusted cages would need to be repainted so your canary doesn't pick at the flakes and become ill. Choose a used cage as you would a new one, considering the size and shape of it, as well as the ease with which it can be cleaned. When you don't know the history of the bird that used

Make sure that the cage bars are not so far apart that the canary can escape or get its head stuck between the bars.

the cage before yours, you want to destroy any germs that might have grown or may have lived on the cage. You should scrub a used cage thoroughly with soap and water, then soak it in or wipe it down with a solution of 10 percent bleach and/or leave it in the sun for several days to disinfect it.

Any cage you choose will be easier to keep clean if you can disassemble it occasionally to scrub it thoroughly. Cage doors come in many shapes and styles as well. Be sure your hand can reach through the door of the cage, and that you can access any part of the cage. Doors can open from the side or slide down "guillotine" style. Since most canaries stay in their cages and don't enter and exit their abodes regularly, you don't necessarily need a large door.

Placing the Cage

One of the important aspects of bringing a canary into your home is where to place the cage. If the canary is happy and comfortable, it will be more likely to sing. If you have easy access to the cage and are able to clean around it, you will be happier! You probably also want to have your canary in a part of your home where you can enjoy its song. A canary can fit in well in the family living room or a dining room. It might enjoy looking at nature from an enclosed porch, and could enjoy a children's playroom if play there doesn't get too rough! Too much noise is distracting to these musically inclined birds, so don't place a canary's cage near a TV or speakers.

Canaries will feel safest if they are at chest level or higher. They are prey animals, and it's disconcerting for them to be looked down on all the time. You can hang a cage for your canary, put a cage on a stand or put it on a piece of furniture. I have done all of the above. If you decide to use a cage stand, be sure it is sturdy and will stay put when household traffic whirls around it. If you put a cage on a piece of furniture, it's wise to cover the top of the furniture with towels or sheets. Cages can scratch the finish of most furniture. You also want to be able to clean behind the furniture because feed and feathers will fly everywhere.

Clean a used cage thoroughly before placing your new canary in it.

It can be dangerous to keep birds in or near the kitchen because they have delicate respiratory systems compared to people, though you can minimize the danger somewhat. Nonstick cookware is lethal to birds if it is overheated. So, if you do use it (or nonstick bakewear, drip pans, or ironing board covers) be aware of overheating. Or you could take my approach, which is not to use it at all. The convenience doesn't seem worth the risk to me. Other dangers in or near kitchens for a canary who happens to be out of its cage are smoke, the possibility of fire, open pans of hot water, sizzling goodies in fry pans and dishwater. Chemicals and fumes also affect birds. Cleaning agents used in a kitchen or bathroom, or fumes from a self-cleaning oven, could be dangerous or deadly for your bird.

Canaries will feel safest placed at chest level or higher—a stand like this one should keep the bird feeling comfortable.

Canaries like to be in light, natural places. They like looking out the window at greenery and native birds, but if their whole cage is exposed to direct sunlight at any time during the day, it would get too hot for them. An appropriate window location would have an awning or porch in front of it, or the window would be covered by curtains or blinds.

Once your canary starts singing, then you've found the spot in your home where it is comfortable. This might take a week or two, as it adjusts to your household and feels secure in its new surroundings. If you think you have an ideal location for a canary, but it doesn't sing, then move it until you are both happy. If your canary doesn't sing because it turns out to be a hen, then you have some decisions to make beyond cage placement. You might want to find a home for it in a classroom where a quiet bird is appreciated, get a mate for it and start raising canaries, place the hen with a breeder, trade it back in for a male, or continue to enjoy the bird's company and cheerful personality even with no song!

Once your canary starts singing, you know you have found the right spot for its cage.

Accessories

Your canary will need some items in its cage for feeding and comfort.

BOWLS

Food bowls might come with your cage. Even so, if you buy an extra set that fits your cage when you purchase it, servicing the cage will be much easier. You can pull out the old bowls, put in the new and clean dirty bowls at your leisure. Flat bowls work best for canaries so that you don't end up with the top layer of seed eaten and hulled and plenty of seed underneath that is not available to your canary. Get some extra dishes, too. You'll want dishes for occasional gravel, dishes for soft food, dishes for song food or dishes for feeding seed separately. Get duplicates of these dishes, too. If you are purchasing dishes that don't come with your cage, be sure they will fit. Certain bar widths and some horizontal bars at correct heights are usually necessary to hang extra feed dishes.

WATER

You can offer your canary water in a water tube or in a small dish. If you offer your canary water in a large dish, it will probably bathe in it. (This is certainly not a bird for which you can put vitamins in the water! They would be a sticky mess.) Water should be changed daily, or more often if you notice that it has gotten soiled. Using bottled water or boiled or filtered tap water is preferable to using water straight out of the tap.

Water bowls tend to get slimy. They should be scrubbed with soap and water daily. Every few days, let them soak for about fifteen minutes in a solution that is one part bleach to nine parts water (for example, 3/4 cup bleach in a gallon of water). For bleach to act as a disinfectant, the bowls need to be washed first, as "organic matter" such as food and droppings impede the process. Soak the bowls in bleach solution for at least ten minutes. You cannot re-use this solution; it needs to be discarded because the bleach breaks down quickly upon exposure to air and light. There are alternative disinfectants available. If you use another one, learn how to discard it properly, and find out if it breaks down in the environment or whether it pollutes water supplies.

PERCHES

Types

It's best for canaries to perch on multidiameter perches, which makes natural branches desirable. This way a canary can change its foot position to avoid getting sore feet. You could use many different kinds of safe branches, including oak, willow and maple. Many kinds of fruit tree branches are fine, too. Manzanita and eucalyptus are favorites of bird owners but may have oils in them that are not beneficial for bird feet on a long-term basis, so only include some of these, with other perches as well. If you gather perches outdoors, pick them up from areas that are some distance from a road, so that the branches won't have exhaust chemicals on them. Once you get the branches home, wipe them off with a 10 percent bleach solution and let them dry, or wash them with soap and water, then let them dry in the sun. You may also bake branches in a low-heat oven to kill pests.

Perches of different diameters and materials will help your canary avoid foot problems.

If you decide to use dowel rods for perches, get several sizes and shapes to give your canary a variety of feet positions. Dowels often come in round, oval and square shapes.

Canaries also enjoy swings. These may be made of dowel rods and have perches protruding from them, or they might be a straight swing you hang from the top of the cage. Many are decorated with colored woods or beads, making your canary's cage a little more cheerful. Whatever the design, swings are a canary favorite. My Skippy sits on his for hours, making it swing from side to side and watching what's happening in the household.

Perch Placement

When placing perches in a cage, be sure that droppings will not fall in the canary's food or water. You may wish to concentrate perches at either end of a cage, making it necessary for your canary to fly and exercise. Other options include half-perches that screw onto the side of a cage, or a branch from a tree or hedge that you secure to the bottom of the cage.

THE BATH

One of the highlights of having a canary as a companion animal is giving it baths. Canaries enjoy bathing, and you'll probably enjoy their enjoyment! Canaries don't climb into a bath and soak. They wade into shallow water that splashes around their ankles, then start flicking water with their beak and eventually go at it with their wings and dip their bodies in the water. You will want to provide large, shallow bathing dishes for your canary. There are many styles of baths made especially for canaries. Some hang on the cage. The budgie baths with mirrors in the bottom work, as does a saucer or a baking pan. Shallow pet bowls are ideal. Be sure to check that your canary has water a few times a day. Baths are more desirable if the weather is hot because they help a canary cool off.

There are many types of canary baths to choose from—your canary will certainly reward you with a show!

Baths should be offered almost daily. If your canary has a chance to dry in the sun afterwards, it will be even happier. If for some reason you have a canary that doesn't bathe frequently, consider misting it with warm water, while continuing to offer it saucers of bath water. It may eventually get the idea. If plain, shallow water doesn't work, try varying the dish in which you present bath water, or try offering your canary wet greens instead of bath water—your bird may prefer to bathe in the residual water on the greens. Some canaries are the "back to nature" types.

CUTTLEBONE

There should be a cuttlebone available to your canary at all times. Throughout much of the year, your pet may not actually eat it, but during the molt or if a hen lays eggs she will need this source of calcium. If a cuttlebone gets soiled, you should replace it. An alternative to offering cuttlebone is offering a mineral block or fine oyster-shell grit. Offer your canary grit and a vitamin supplement several times a month. Sprinkle dry vitamins on its moist fresh vegetables, using a salt shaker filled with dry, powdered avian vitamins.

Toys

Your canary may enjoy some toys and some entertainment to liven up its life. The toys should be parakeet-sized, bright, colorful and glittery. Toys with colorful and/or movable beads and pieces of sisal to pull are favorites. Canaries don't chew, so not all parakeet or small parrot toys are appealing to a canary. Any kind of little perch or swing your canary can land on would be appreciated. Canaries really enjoy grooming or pulling at a toy that consists of bristles held together. Their natural nest building instinct comes into play with this toy, I think. Nesting canaries weave strips of material into a bowl shape for a loose, open nest, much like our wild robins. Entertainment beyond toys consists of music, a view of outside birds, the company of other companion birds inside and maybe even some free-flight time.

Canary-Proofing Your Home

Make your living space temporarily "canary-proof" if you let your bird fly for exercise. Be aware that there is always a danger of escape or injury if you let your canary fly free in your home. If you can provide your canary with a free-flight aviary as a living environment, this is preferable.

If you do allow your canary free flight in your home, take precautions to make your home safe. Close the blinds or curtains covering windows, so your bird does not try to fly through them. For the same reason, cover mirrors, as these look like open spaces to birds. Any open, deep water is dangerous to birds. If a bird flies into a sink or toilet, it usually can't get out. It's made to fly, not swim. Soapy water is especially dangerous, as it destroys the natural oils in a bird's feathers that help to keep it waterproof and to use its feathers as insulation to stay warm. Of course,

Canaries allowed to fly around the home can learn to return to their cages.

doors and windows should be closed or safely screened when your bird is out.

If you have a free-flying canary, you don't want to have poisonous houseplants available for it to peck at. A canary isn't as curious or destructive as a parrot, but it might be tempted by greens. Christmas favorites are poisonous: holly, mistletoe and poinsettia. Poisonous houseplants include diffenbachia, while usually ficus trees, jade, palms, ferns and succulents are safe.

If you have dog or cat, make sure they are safely in another room while the canary is out. No matter how well behaved they are normally, the fast actions of a canary loose in the room would be tempting to these natural predators.

Your Convenience

Some items are not absolutely necessary for a canary's health but may make your work easier. You may consider placing an air purifier near a bird cage, especially if there are people in the family with allergies. One canary does not create a lot of dust or mess, but if you have several birds in the household, it is something to consider. Once people get involved in the hobby of keeping birds and set aside a room just for their birds, they usually do have an air purifier.

Lighting

Another aspect of your bird's environment is lighting. A bird benefits greatly from direct sunlight, but it is not always possible to make this available to our pets. An alternative is the use of "full-spectrum" lighting, which has all the rays of sunlight; our normal incandescent and fluorescent lighting does not. Sunlight shining through a window is not beneficial either, as the rays are filtered by window glass.

Birds benefit from full-spectrum lighting because it helps them manufacture vitamin D and metabolize calcium in their diets. For our enjoyment, full-spectrum lighting shows off the real colors of birds. You will enjoy your vibrantly colored canary that much more with this type of lighting. Traditional full-spectrum bulbs are fluorescent tubes, which can be hung with shop lights from the ceiling or along a wall close to a bird cage or aviary. There are alternative bulbs and lamps available now. Shop for them at a pet store, reptile supply provider, bird mart, in bird magazines or a bird supply catalog. You can ask about the availability of full-spectrum bulbs at a lighting store in your area. They are sometimes supplied to offices to encourage peak performance and minimum eye strain for people who work under artificial lighting all day.

Studies have shown that canaries sing most lustily and freely when day and night are clearly distinct. Use a dark cover at night over your canary's cage, and light its living area during the day to provide a strong sense of day and night.

The use of dimmers and timers to control lighting is a definite advantage in bird keeping. Ideal lighting for keeping a canary is fourteen hours of daylight a day. In the U.S., our hours of daylight vary throughout the year. With a timer, you can create a consistent lighted environment for your bird.

The use of lighting timers can keep your canary singing year-round.

If you use dimmers, as well as timers, you can create dusk before night. These are items available at your local hardware or lighting store. They also serve as theft deterrents when you are out of town, keeping your home lit and lights going on and off normally despite your absence.

Storing Feed

Pests certainly like the same kind of food that canaries do. Moths and moth larvae are attracted to seed and feed. If the larvae are in feed, they create a "webby" feed. They don't actually do any harm to your bird, which could get a little extra protein in its diet from eating insect larvae, but usually the resulting white moths are bothersome to have in a home.

You can prevent the growth of any larvae that might be in feed by making it a practice to freeze any food you purchase for your bird for at least twenty-four hours before opening the bag. Also, keeping the area around your cage or aviaries clean prevents the growth of the next generation of moths. Once your seed or feed has been frozen, it's best to store it in a dry, airtight container so no pests can get into it.

The other kind of food contamination to prevent is the growth of mold and bacteria. Feed and seed keep longer if they are kept dry and cool. On a sticky summer day, this could be a challenge! You can keep your feed in the refrigerator, or take small amounts at a time out of the freezer if you have room to do so. Two simple habits will help prevent the growth of mold and bacteria. One is washing out your food container after you empty it. By doing so, you ensure that all of the old feed is gone instead of remaining to grow bacteria. Another good habit is to have a cup or scoop in your food container. To feed your bird, use the scoop to fill its feed dishes instead of dipping the potentially soiled dishes into the feed. This keeps your food supply as clean and bacteria-free as you can possibly make it.

Predators

Although you probably aren't too worried about cobras in your household, more mundane pests such as mice and rats come looking for handouts. You'll want to keep your feed in rodent-proof as well as moth-proof containers. These might range from sealed plastic containers to glass jars or metal canisters. In keeping with making bird keeping pleasing as well as practical, you can choose pretty containers or wall-mounted dispensers.

Mice and rats can cause problems in aviaries, as their droppings are loaded with bacteria. They can frighten caged birds, and, of course, larger rats may even harm a bird or chicks.

If you know you have rodents in or near your bird's enclosure, you should aggressively try to discourage them. The best way to discourage rodents is not to feed them. Take out feed cups and clean up well in the evening before your birds settle down. Make cages, aviaries and bird rooms as rodent-proof as possible. Underground wire, cement flooring or aluminum flashing can be used to protect a well-planned, rodent-proof aviary. Usually rodent protection has to extend underground, as these animals burrow or live in walls.

Of course you can also trap rodents, in traditional snap traps, glue traps or humane live traps. Peanut butter is a better bait than cheese, despite media portrayals. There is poison available that will kill rodents, which shouldn't be placed anywhere near a bird's enclosure.

You can keep a cat who is a good mouser. A cat that has learned to hunt may also be interested in canaries, so consider this last move carefully! I know of one aviary that raises bird-friendly cats for their rodent patrol, but often the small size and quick actions of canaries are more than a cat can resist.

If you keep a cat as a mouser, beware that it doesn't become too interested in your canaries as well!

Other pests are more common in outside aviaries than inside, including raccoons, opossums and birds of prey. In some areas, snakes are a concern. In all cases, a good aviary design thwarts pests, as does knowing enough about their habits to prevent creating an inviting situation for them.

While we're talking about predatory snakes, a canary was involved in the discovery of King Tut's tomb. There was a legendary curse protecting the tombs of Egypt's mummified kings. A gentleman by the name of Howard Carter braved the curse to search for one of these archaeologically rich finds. To liven up his household during his search, he bought a canary and kept it in a gilded cage. One of his servants is purported to have exclaimed, "It's a bird of gold that will bring luck. This year we will find a tomb full of gold." Within that week, Carter did indeed find a tomb originally called "the tomb of the Golden Bird."

Good aviary design should keep pests out and your canaries in!

That's extraordinary enough, but the canary did not escape the mummy's curse. On the day Howard Carter discovered the tomb of Tutankhamen, a cobra entered his house and swallowed the hapless golden canary. The cobra is not a common snake in Egypt, but it is the symbol of royalty, a symbol a pharaoh wore upon his forehead. The patron of the expedition died some five months later of blood poisoning from an infected mosquito bite. To some, it appeared the tomb's curse was indeed invoked.

Keeping Clean

Develop good daily cleaning habits to keep your bird healthy and its environment pleasant to both of you. To start the day, full-spectrum lights would go on via a timer. This helps your canary process vitamin D. Shortly before or after the lights are on, you would uncover your canary's cage so it can be in the light and enjoy another full, exciting day as a member of your household.

If your cage has a wire grid in the bottom, wipe this clean or scrape it clean. If you do this task daily, you will have less work to do to keep it clean than if you wait to do a major cleaning.

CAGE BOTTOMS

Change cage papers and sweep stray feed, seed and feathers from around the cage area. It is easier in a busy household to layer cage papers, then roll one up and discard it. Though it may be tempting to use something other than paper to line the bottom of the cage, it is not recommended. With any of the crumbled, ground or pelleted cage floor covering, you may be tempted to wait a day or two before cleaning your canary's cage, giving molds and bacteria time to grow in discarded food and droppings. Another point is that some cage bottom materials are appealing to a bird to eat but aren't edible. They either block up their digestive tract or swell up in it. It's better not to offer the temptation.

> ### KEEP YOUR BIRD'S HOME TIDY
>
> It is important to keep a bird in clean, sanitary surroundings. With their sensitive respiratory systems, the most likely maladies for canaries are respiratory infections resulting from molds and bacteria in their environment. In addition, too much scattered seed around a pet bird could attract pests you do not want to host, such as moths, insects and mice.
>
> Aside from the health issues, there is your responsibility to a bird you choose to keep in a cage. A caged bird depends on you to provide it with everything that a wild bird would have naturally—sunlight, rain, perches and food.

Another good thing about paper linings and daily care is that you have a chance to monitor your canary's droppings. If something is amiss, you'll spot it within a few hours. Daily inspection means that you'll be aware of what your canary's "normal" droppings look like!

The paper you use can be newspaper, paper toweling or recycled computer paper. Some newspapers sell "end rolls," which are unprinted newsprint paper that come on large rolls. Many newspapers are now printed with nontoxic soy inks and are safe for use around our birds. To find out, call your local paper and ask to talk to the press foreman. Butcher paper is waterproofed on one side and handy for bird paper. You could also use paper bags as cage liners.

Food Preparation

Prepare the day's food in your second set of dishes. Fill a dish with fresh seed and another dish with a conditioning food containing vitamins, or feed a manufactured diet (but no vitamins). A separate dish or clip should be for fresh fruit, greens and vegetables.

Remove the dishes from the day before and replace them with today's clean, newly filled dishes. Instead of providing a full seed cup, provide enough seed or feed for about a day and discard what's left. Cleanliness and hygiene are top priorities. Remove the contents of the old dishes and put the dishes in a dishtub or the dishwasher so they can be cleaned.

In the evening, remove the dish or clip that held soft foods (the ones used for greens or sprouts). If your canary is molting and you are feeding it egg food, you should probably only leave the food in the cage for a short time in the morning and remove what wasn't eaten. Eggs spoil quickly. Again in the evening, change soiled water.

If you like, offer your canary an afternoon snack. Refill its food dish and offer it some song food or molting food. You could give it a treat like a dandelion leaf from your lawn or a fresh edible flower from your garden. My canaries have always enjoyed nasturtiums. I just have to remind myself of what I've fed them when I change their papers next. Red flowers lead to red droppings.

Water Dispensers

Remove your bird's drinking tube or water dish. Wash it with soap and water, fill it with fresh bottled or filtered water then place it back in the cage. You can efficiently clean most water tubes with a stiff bottle brush. Of course, you could have a duplicate for this item, as well. Every few days also disinfect the water dish in a 10 percent bleach solution (nine parts water to one part bleach) for at least ten minutes; rinse the water dish then replace it.

BATH TIME

Almost daily, offer your canary a bath in a shallow dish. On some cold mornings this may not be appropriate. With bird chores taken care of, turn on soft music for the music-appreciating member of your family. This is especially welcomed by your bird if you will be gone during the day.

OBSERVE YOUR BIRD

Take some time daily to observe your bird. Are its toenails getting long and need to be cut? Does it have crusty eyes, nostrils or feet? Is it active and perky? Is it singing? Is your bird molting, signaling to you that it might need dietary supplementation and a few weeks of quiet?

In the evening, about fourteen hours after you have uncovered your canary's cage, it's time to cover it again. The lights can be turned off, or should go off on a timer near the same time. The cycle is starting over!

Clean water tubes with a bottle brush daily.

Weekly Care

Once a week, consider letting your canary out for some flight time if your house is safe for it. Also clean your canary's cage thoroughly once a week. Take it apart and scrub it with soap and water. Vacuum or sweep around the cage. If your canary is molting and those feathers refuse to be swept tamely, spritz them with a little water. Rinse off your cage and dry it thoroughly. If it's a sunny day, this job will be easy. If

*Take note of
your bird's con-
dition daily—
this canary
needs its toe-
nails trimmed.*

you don't want your canary to fly about during this
time, your smaller travel cage will come in handy.
When the whole cage is once again clean and ready to
be inhabited, put your canary companion back into it.
You're ready for another week.

Seasonal Changes

Of course, in the dead of winter you aren't going to
offer your canary dandelion leaves for treats. For a pet
singing canary, the main seasonal event each year is
the molt. If you are color-feeding your canary, you will
want to obtain color food and feed it prior to and during its molt, which will probably happen some time
between June and September. Growing new feathers
takes extra protein, so feeding a canary nesting food or
an egg food daily is a good idea at this time. At the
least, mash a little hard cooked egg for your bird.

Emergency Preparedness

It is a good idea to have a carrier when you own a bird
in case there's ever a home emergency that requires
that you flee the house FAST! If you ever need to exit
your house because of an emergency, and can't get to
your carrier or spare cage, remember a pillow case will
contain your canary nicely in such a time. Carriers also
are great to have for trips to the veterinarian or maybe
even a classroom visit. It's also possible that a smaller
cage is appropriate to travel with on vacation if you

take your canary with you. It's nice to have a "spare" for when you do deep-down cleaning, too.

It's always advisable to have extra food and water on hand. Disaster can happen at any time. You might consider writing down your wishes for your canary also, in case you should ever be in an accident. Let a family member or special friend know what those wishes are. If you intend to pass your canary on to an acquaintance or relative, be sure the new owner would want it. Life is truly uncertain; it never hurts to be prepared. In the meantime, you are thoroughly enjoying your canary, and without a doubt it is making each day special!

chapter 6

Feeding and Grooming a Canary

Feeding a canary using a traditional seed diet with supplements can be time-consuming but is still widespread among canary fanciers. Canary diet does tend to vary with the seasons as well. If you have a color-fed canary, you will want to provide it with a color supplement before and during its molt to keep the lovely red, orange or bronze you prize. Molting canaries and breeding canaries have special requirements to maintain optimum health.

Formulated Diets

There are manufactured diets available that provide our caged birds with a selection of the vitamins and minerals they need. Thus, balanced, good nutrition is found in every bite, and many diet manufacturers make formulated diets in a small size that canaries can eat. Finding a supply of formulated diet, converting a seed-eating bird to it and offering sufficient variety in your bird's daily fare then become your challenges.

Formulated diets are available at pet stores, feed stores, bird marts and through mail-order catalogs. Be sure to get the right size diet for your canary. Larger diets don't crush, they turn into powder. To ensure that you have a supply of food available when you need it, consider feeding two different kinds of formulated diet. You never know when a merchant may run out of one brand. It is also a good idea to keep some feed stocked in the freezer or refrigerator.

> ### BENEFITS OF A FORMULATED DIET
>
> - Adequate nutrition improves a bird's health.
>
> - Less mess, with no seed hulls.
>
> - Safer than feeding foods that spoil quickly (like egg food).
>
> - Less waste.
>
> - All known nutritional needs are contained in every bite of food (protein, carbohydrates, fat, vitamins, minerals).

I found that my canaries readily accepted a formulated diet, and no conversion was involved. That might not be the case with your canary. If your canary was raised on a seed diet, it might not recognize that the diet you are offering it is food. For this reason, it doesn't usually work to offer seed and a new formulated diet at the same time. The bird chooses what it knows is food, which is the seed it is used to eating. If you convert your bird to a manufactured diet, there are several tactics you can use. Simply removing a bird's seed and offering a different diet does not work. You do not want to starve your avian companion; you want to do what is best for its health in the long run.

When I converted birds to a formulated diet, I took away seeds during the day and only left formulated diet in the cage. Then in the evening they got some seed. It didn't take long for them to peck at the formulate diet out of curiosity and eventually eat it. Once a few birds had discovered that this stuff was food, others quickly

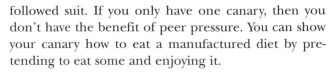

*Manufactured
foods, such as
these pellets,
can offer your
canary a good,
balanced diet.*

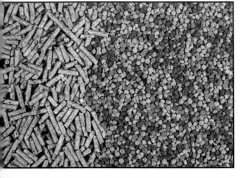

*Seed-based diets
should be sup-
plemented with
vitamins and
minerals.*

followed suit. If you only have one canary, then you don't have the benefit of peer pressure. You can show your canary how to eat a manufactured diet by pretending to eat some and enjoying it.

To stimulate your bird to try a new diet, sprinkle a few pellets on a canary's veggies or put some in a dish, sprinkle with lemon juice or fruit juice. Bake them into bird bread so the diet is incognito. Once you have a canary that eats a formulated diet, your maintenance will be much lower and cleanup will be easier. You will also know that you are doing the best you can to properly feed your bird.

There is a caution to remember. If you feed a seed-based diet, it should be supplemented with vitamins because seeds lack some essential nutrients. If your canary eats a formulated diet, do not offer vitamins. Though some vitamins are good, more are not better!

DIET STORAGE AND USE

Formulated diets may come in a package larger than you can use in a couple weeks. You can safely refrigerate the diet to store it, or even freeze part of it to maintain its freshness. Be sure to store the diet in dry, airtight and vermin-proof containers. When you have emptied a container, wash it and dry it before refilling it. That way you aren't mixing older diet with new, avoiding any problem with mold or bacteria.

Remember, too, to avoid contamination by using a cup or scoop to fill food dishes. Don't ever dip the dishes into a container of feed. There are all kinds of convenient containers for feed that keep it dry, dispense it or allow you to see how much you have.

Fresh Treats

Whether you feed a seed-based diet or a formulated diet to your canary, greens, fruit and vegetable treats should be a regular part of what you feed. They do not contribute a great deal of calories to a bird's daily intake, but they are a diversion, enjoyable for the bird and offer it variety in its diet. You may offer a canary various fresh foods, including apples, broccoli, canned corn, carrots, chickweed, chicory, comfrey, dandelion greens, grape halves, leaf lettuce, nasturtium blossoms, orange, peas, spinach, squash and sweet potatoes. This list is by no means complete, and it doesn't represent the many ways in which you can present food.

Canaries usually are fed more vegetables than fruit but will enjoy bits of whatever fruit is in season. Remember that they can't break up large pieces of food, so cut fruits with tough skins. I offer my canary grape halves, for example, and they manage to eat a slice of apple or orange and leave only the skin. To feed carrot, sweet potato or squash, you could microwave it until it is soft, or finely grate it for your canary. You may boil seeds and carrots together for your birds as a treat, then freeze what you don't use right away. Other foods can be microwaved, cut, chopped, grated or baked into treat bread. If you have frozen vegetables to feed, such as peas and corn, thaw them under hot running water to present to your canaries. Many of the deep green vegetables, including dandelion greens, are highly nutritious. Carrots and squash contain carotene and, along with red peppers, are a natural color food.

> ## NUTRITIOUS SPROUTS
>
> You can turn seeds into a healthier treat by sprouting them. Soak a regular seed mix or a legume like mung beans (the bean sprouts we use in Chinese cooking) in water for twenty-four hours. To control the growth of mold I add a couple drops of either bleach or a natural grapefruit-derived fungal inhibitor from a health food store. After twenty-four hours, rinse the seeds and put them in a strainer. Keep them in a dark place and continue rinsing them several times a day. As sprouts develop, put them in the light and green sprouts will develop. You can refrigerate them for a few days. If mold develops at any time or the seeds smell bad, don't feed them to your birds. The length of time for sprouting varies with the temperature and with the seed or legume you are sprouting.

The Traditional Seed Diet

For centuries, canaries have been fed seeds. There are numerous companies making products to aid you in feeding your canary. If you are set on carrying on this seed-diet tradition, here are some of the basics.

The seed-based canary diet consists of a mixture of canary seed and millet, both high in carbohydrates, and other high-fat seeds such as hemp, rape and niger. When their staple diet is seed, canaries should be fed greens and receive a powdered vitamin or a condition food containing vitamins.

YUMMY PELLET MUFFINS!

When a bird has another bird to show it that a formulated diet is food, it often converts quickly. Other ways to entice your bird to eat formulated diet is to dress up the crumbles in some way. A simple bird bread can be made with a package of corn muffin mix. You can add manufactured diet to it, grate carrots in the bread, bake the recipe with an extra egg or make it with a jar of baby food for extra vitamins. If you're sure no one will sneak a bite, it's healthy for your birds to have crushed egg shells in the batter.

Breeders also usually supplement the canary diet with egg food for breeding birds. A canary going through the molt will also benefit from an increase in protein in its diet. It has a lot of new feathers to grow. Though there are numerous recipes for egg food, there are also commercial egg biscuits and conditioning supplements for your canary. The combination many canary breeders feed is hard-boiled egg, dried bread crumbs, grated carrot and wheat germ. Other mixtures contain vitamin supplements. Here are two food supplement recipes published by bird clubs:

Canary Condition Food

- 2 cups crushed wheat flakes or corn flakes
- 2 cups Gerber's Hi-Protein baby cereal flakes
- 2 cups commercial condition food (optional)
- 1 cup boiled, oven-dried, crushed egg shells
- 1 cup rape seed or canary song food
- 1 level tablespoon powdered bird vitamin

Mix and store in cool place. Feed to molting or breeding birds as a source of extra protein and calcium.

Traditional Egg Food

- 1 dozen hard-boiled eggs
- 1 tablespoon of powdered bird vitamin
- 2 packages unflavored gelatin
- 7 cups Gerber's Hi-Protein baby cereal flakes
- 5 cups crushed bread
- 1 heaping teaspoon brewer's yeast

Mix, place in baggies and freeze until ready for use. This recipe feeds twenty birds for three months. Adjust if you have fewer birds!

Molting Diet

The time of the year when you should supplement a canary's diet with extra protein is when it is molting. This usually happens once a year, lasts four to five weeks and occurs sometime between June and September. Males usually stop singing when they are molting, which is the process of gradually and systematically losing their old feathers and growing in new ones. For canaries, the head feathers are the last to grow in.

Young canaries, during their first year, may change color slightly as they attain their adult plumage. Young birds do not replace their tail and long wing "flight" feathers during their first molt. In the show world, these birds are called "unflighted."

Your molting canaries will appreciate their baths more than ever. This is also a good time to keep your canary warm and stress free. Offer it extra nutrients from oily niger, flax and rape seed, as well as egg food or a nestling food.

Your main job, besides making your molting canary comfortable, is sweeping up feathers, which fairly rain down from a molting bird. This is a stressful time of year for your canary, but with general good health and a little extra attention and feeding from you, you will both be fine when it's over, and your canary will have a glistening new set of feathers.

Color-Feeding Canaries

Some red-orange canaries have the ability to metabolize pro-vitamin A into their natural color, so that they turn various shades of red. Canaries with the genetic ability to metabolize red pigment are called Red factor canaries. These canaries get red pigment from their diet. If you've ever been to a zoo, you may have seen flamingos that were more white than pink. They also need dietary supplements to retain their rich pink color.

Red factor canaries can be fed color food to enhance the pigment in their feathers.

The brightest red canaries are fed a color supplement. Look for one that is a mixture of the synthetic pigment canthaxanthin and beta-carotene. Any other ingredients are just fillers. The use of canthaxanthin alone produces a duller shade of brick red in your canaries, while the mixture produces bright red.

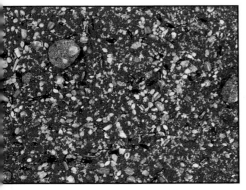

Canary breeders with Red factor birds must color-feed their nesting hens so that the hens, in turn, color-feed their chicks. Just before a pet canary's molt and during its molt, it should be fed this supplement in order to develop a deep, rich red, if you wish to do so. Carotene is found naturally in carrots and red cayenne pepper, paprika, beets, berries, cherries, grated carrots, sweet potatoes, squash and tomatoes. You will attain a soft shade of orange on your bird merely by having these foods in its diet.

To color-feed canaries, powdered carotene-canthaxanthin is mixed with water and kept in the refrigerator. The ratio of mix to water is 1 teaspoon per ½ gallon of water. It will stay viable for one week if you keep it in the refrigerator. Before and throughout the molt, this should be the only water available. The youngest canaries, who do not molt their flight feathers, will retain light-colored tail and flight feathers unless they were color-fed as nestlings, while the rest of their feathers color. In ensuing years, all of their feathers will change color.

Another product available for color-feeding is orange carotenoids in an oil base. A teaspoon of the oil can be added to a pound of treat seed like thistle or hemp, allowed to soak in overnight and then fed occasionally as a treat in addition to the water color supplement.

Look in bird magazines and specialty catalogs for sources of color-feeding supplements. The color-bred canary societies and specialty breeders should also be able to direct you to sources of the pigment.

Grooming Your Canary

Besides attention to its molt and to its color, a canary occasionally needs attention to its grooming. You already know that you need to offer your canary a bath regularly. Canaries do not need and should not have their wings clipped. They need the exercise they derive from flying about their cage, aviary or a room.

The grooming a canary needs most often is toenail clipping. In the lightest canaries with white toenails, it is easy

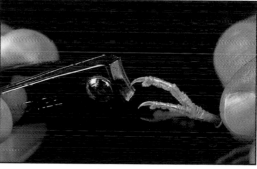

Be careful not to clip too far into the nail when clipping toenails.

to see the blood vessels of the living part of the bird's nails. You should clip just the tip of a canary's nail. This is the grown-out part that does not contain nerves or a blood supply. If you do cause a toenail to bleed, apply some styptic powder from a pet store or apply pressure by holding the nail in a bar of soap. At last, a use for that collection from your travels! Flour or corn starch also work as a last resort, though not as quickly or as efficiently as styptic powder.

Nail clipping is required every few weeks, and makes perching much easier for your bird. There is some danger of untended canary nails curling under and starting to grow into a bird's foot, creating infection.

You can clip your canary's nails easily. You begin by catching it. I use my hands; you may wish to use a net. Canaries are not aggressive birds; they won't bite you when you catch them. In fact, they grow limp and quiet. It's a really unsettling experience the first time! Hold the canary cupped in your fingers, without compressing its chest. Canaries don't have a muscular diaphragm to help them continue breathing as we do. Their chest wall needs to be free to expand so they can breathe. Use your fingers, or get help from an assistant, to hold out the canary's toes and clip its nails one by one. I use a nail clipper designed for human nails; nail scissors would also work. If you can't see well at this close range, or even if you're just squeamish, a pet store bird groomer or your veterinarian will clip toenails for you. There may also be a bird club member who does bird grooming.

Canaries are not aggressive birds and will not bite when caught.

While you have your canary at close range, check that it has not caught any fibers around its leg or toes, that its eyes and nostrils are clear and that its vent is clean. If you have a canary with long, wide feathers, you may need to trim the feathers around its vent so it is more tidy.

Move slowly and hold your canary gently during the nail trimming process, reassuring it that you are only caring for it. Then release your pet back into its cage, and the incident will be quickly forgotten.

chapter 7

Your Canary's Health

It is my hope you will be able to take your canary to see an avian veterinarian at an appropriate time after reading about disease symptoms in this chapter. Canaries have their own pox virus called Canary pox. Some of the wide, soft-feathered breeds are especially prone to feather lumps and respiratory diseases.

Some canary diseases are preventable through husbandry. Of course, any bird may have accidents. The best you can do for your canary is to know what to do in the event of an emergency, work at keeping it safe by minimizing danger and stay in touch with a good avian veterinarian so you know where to take it when there is a need for medical assistance.

Recognizing Illness

If you determine that your bird is ill, it should be separated from other birds and be kept warm. You can fashion a temporary "hospital cage" by wrapping towels around a small cage and placing a light bulb at one end.

The bird can regulate the amount of heat it wants by moving closer or further from the light bulb. An infrared lamp or a heat lamp will work even better. Alternatively, you could put a canary in a box and put a heating pad under part of the box, again so the canary can move to a temperature that is comfortable for it.

Also, be sure the canary has access to food and water. If your canary is on the bottom of the cage, you should place bowls there for it. If it is perching, place seed near its location in the cage. When a bird is ill, offer its favorite treats, without worrying whether they are good for it or not. Does your canary relish canned corn, egg food or apples? Offer them now.

If your canary is hurt, you do not want it to do further damage to itself. Keep the bird in a semidark area, and keep activity around it to a minimum. Once your ill or hurt canary is comfortable, you can call your avian veterinarian for further advice. Be sure to supply as many details as possible. What has your canary been eating? How long has it acted like this? Did it fly into something or display other symptoms? Was another animal involved? All of these things are clues to a veterinarian on how to treat your bird to restore its health or to make it more comfortable.

An illness or accident may not occur during normal business hours. Do you know the policy of your

---

SICK BIRDS

Some of the symptoms of a sick bird are:

- lack of singing
- lower level of activity
- puffed up appearance
- sitting on the bottom of the cage
- crustiness around the eyes and mouth
- pumping tail
- open-mouthed or labored breathing
- untidy appearance
- swellings
- messy vent area
- whole seeds passed in the droppings

veterinarian about emergencies? Do you know of an emergency clinic or an alternate veterinarian available in the off-hours? This is information you should keep handy.

Be sure to get to know an avian veterinarian before you need one desperately, as in an emergency. Birds are very different from dogs and cats, and not all veterinarians have taken the time or attended additional courses in order to be versed in their care.

Visiting an Avian Veterinarian

The best way to find an avian veterinarian in your area is to get a referral from a local bird owner. Contact someone in a bird club, ask a bird owner who is happy with his or her veterinarian or ask for a referral from a veterinarian who does not treat birds. You can also contact the Association of Avian Veterinarians or search their Web site for a listing of avian veterinarians. You will be most comfortable with your bird's veterinarian if you schedule an initial "well bird" visit when you get your new canary. This means that you will take your bird in to see the veterinarian before you notice any signs or symptoms of illness. This way the veterinarian will know what is the normal state of health for your particular bird and will be better able to tell when it is ill.

> ### FINDING A VETERINARIAN
>
> To find an avian veterinarian in your area, contact:
>
> Association of Avian Veterinarians
> P.O. Box 811720
> Boca Raton FL 33481
> (561) 393 8901
> aavctrlofc@aol.com

What Happens at the Veterinarian?

If you expect something like a doctor's visit or a trip to the vet with your dog or cat, you might have certain expectations. Things are different with birds. Birds are prey animals (unlike dogs, cats or people), and so they tend not to show symptoms of illness as obviously. An avian veterinarian relies on his or her knowledge of how you care for your canary, its weight over time and lab tests of blood and droppings to assess the health of your pet bird. A veterinarian sees many birds, and his or her visual assessment is an important indicator about the health of your canary. Your observations as the bird's constant companion are also important. Is your canary behaving abnormally, or are things going along okay?

Even when your canary is healthy, it would benefit from a trip to an avian veterinarian—this will allow the veterinarian to get to know what is normal for your bird before there is a problem (Red factor).

It will be in your best interest to answer your veterinarian's questions. They allow a veterinarian to assess a bird's condition much better and may lead to some suggestions for changes in care or routine. If you are visiting your veterinarian because your canary has eaten something that might endanger it, or because there has been an accident, give your veterinarian as much information as possible. Bring in a piece of what the canary ate, or a bottle listing the contents, if that's applicable. For an accident, be clear about the time it happened, your canary's reaction and subsequent symptoms.

Listen to what your veterinarian has to say. What kind of questions do you have for him or her? You should find out what services are available to you. What if you have an emergency outside of office hours? What if your veterinarian goes on vacation? Does your prospective veterinarian refer cases to another veterinarian or have an emergency hot line? What are payment terms? It's reassuring to know whether he or she is committed to ongoing education. Does he or she attend professional meetings or belong to the Association of Avian Veterinarians? Is he or she willing to consult with expert veterinarians if symptoms are puzzling?

Don't be surprised if your bird's veterinarian frequently has new suggestions for you, or if new treatments or tests become available. The level of veterinarian care for bird health is growing at a rapid rate, and there are continually exciting new developments in avian health care.

In addition to lab tests, parasite control and patching up the occasional accident victim, your veterinarian probably offers other services. Your veterinarian can groom your canary's nails and may offer boarding services for when you will be out of town. Often, a veterinarian's office becomes a central point of communication for the community. The office may be notified of lost and found birds, pet sitting services, behavioral consultants, bird club meetings, adoption services and community education projects or requests. You have a lot to gain and a lot to learn by visiting your bird veterinarian on a regular basis!

QUESTIONS AN AVIAN VETERINARIAN MAY ASK

- Canary's sex and breed?
- Band number(s)?
- Canary color and markings?
- Type and size of cage/aviary it lives in?
- Type of perches offered?
- How often is the cage cleaned?
- What type of food is supplied regularly?
- Normal activity/singing?
- How long have you had this canary?
- Do you have other birds?
- Where did you get this canary?
- Do you have other canaries?
- Does anyone in your household smoke?
- Does your canary live inside or outside?

VACCINATIONS

We give our dogs and cats yearly vaccines against life-threatening diseases. Most birds do not receive vaccines. There is a canary pox vaccine, but it may not be appropriate for your pet canary if it is not exposed to other birds. Ask your veterinarian if you are concerned about this.

Preventing Disease and Injury

There are a few basic things you can do to prevent canaries from having accidents and from contracting transmissible diseases. These things may still happen, but at least you have taken as many precautions as possible.

CLEANLINESS

Most canaries will not need vaccinations. Here, a colony of Glosters enjoy their outside aviary.

When you keep birds, cleanliness cannot be stressed enough. Keeping their quarters clean prevents yeast, mold and bacterial infections. It promotes resistance to infection and good health. Cleanliness applies to food sources, bowls, daily cage cleaning, the occasional good cage scrubbing and offering your bird water in a clean cup. Soap and water, a vacuum, a broom and an air purifier are good aids to cleanliness. Disinfecting bowls occasionally with a 10 percent bleach solution is advisable.

NUTRITION

Your canary needs a good diet, based on either a formulated diet or a seed-based diet with supplements and vitamins. Eating right is the best way for it to ward off infection and avoid accidents. Be sure to offer some high-protein foods during a canary's molt to help it grow in new feathers.

CAT BITES

If a cat should scratch or bite your canary, this is an emergency and an immediate trip to the veterinarian is advised. Cats have bacteria in their mouth that multiplies rapidly in a bird's bloodstream, causing death in as little as twenty-four hours. Your avian veterinarian will be able to administer antibiotics to save the bird's life.

Because both dogs and cats are bird predators, supervise their time with a canary, or restrain or separate the two kinds of pets when a canary is out for free-flight time.

Minimize Exposure to Mosquitoes

Mosquitoes can transmit Canary pox to your canary. If you have outside accommodations for your birds, the aviary should be well screened. In your home, put screens on your windows and doors.

Wild Birds

Do not permit wild birds to enter your bird's living area, if possible. Sparrows may transmit lice, mites or diseases to your canaries.

Windows, Mirrors, Doors

If your canary is flying happily around the house, be aware that it could try to fly through a window or into a mirror. Cover these when a bird is flying in the house. Also close doors carefully, in case your bird is tagging along behind you.

Fumes

Canaries are especially susceptible to fumes and smoke. A canary should not be exposed to car exhaust because of the carbon monoxide fumes. Keep canaries away from any chemical you may use. This includes chemicals used for cleaning, for home hair permanents and the fumes from newly laid carpeting as well. Some rug freshener powders and some scented candles are also dangerous. Fumes from a self-cleaning oven can kill a bird. Take your bird to a pet sitter for a day if you decide to operate your oven's self-cleaning feature. Especially lethal are

---

PLANT PATROL

Don't allow your canary to chew on poisonous plants. Common poisonous and safe plants are listed below.

Poisonous Plants

- diffenbachia
- poinsettia
- holly
- mistletoe
- rhubarb leaves

Safe Plants
- ferns
- ficus tree
- jade
- succulents

overheated nonstick surfaces. If a nonstick pan is accidentally overheated, the fumes can kill household birds in minutes. If you overheat a nonstick pan, quickly ventilate the area and take your bird to see a veterinarian if it shows any signs of illness. Nonstick surfaces may also be on ironing boards, ironing board covers, stove drip pans and some bakeware.

Supervise your bird when it must be around other household pets—close contact like this is not recommended.

ACCIDENTS

A common canary accident is getting fiber wound around its leg and foot. Avoid putting fiber into your canary's cage. Supply it with burlap for nests; get sisal, not fabric or rope toys for it. If fiber should get wound around your canary's leg, you may not be able to disentangle, tease off or cut the fiber. It is a job for your veterinarian.

Disease

AIR SAC MITES

If your canary breathes with its mouth open, it may have mites infesting its trachea or further down in its respiratory system. Your avian veterinarian will be able to treat your bird.

ASPERGILLOSIS

This disease is caused by the fungus aspergillus. It is a widespread mold in our environment, often found in moldy, dusty or damp seed. It causes an infection of the lungs and air sacs, and is usually debilitating and fatal. Signs of aspergillosis are weight loss, vomiting and respiratory infection. Keeping your bird's food fresh is a good way to prevent this disorder.

Canary Pox

Canary pox is a viral disease, characterized by blisters or crusts on the skin of a bird around its eyes or on its legs and feet. It can be fatal, but some birds recover. Limiting exposure to mosquitoes and quarantining new birds are good ways to prevent this disease.

External Parasites

Canaries can be infested by fleas, mites and lice. Lice usually live on a bird's feathers. Air sac mites infect the respiratory tract of canaries, while red mites hide in wood and attack birds at night. This causes loss of blood, loss of sleep and can result in feather plucking.

Feather Cysts

Feather cysts are cheesy lumps on a canary's wing, typically found in the large, loose-feathered canaries. It is not known if feather cysts are a genetic or viral problem. Feather cysts usually do not appear until a canary is several years old, and they may continue to appear on a bird. Breeds prone to feather cysts include the Norwich, crested varieties, frilled birds and the dimorphic color-bred canaries. Treatment varies from removal to draining.

Get to know your bird's healthy behavior so that you can quickly recognize symptoms if a problem occurs (Cinnamon Fife).

Feather Plucking

In canaries, feather plucking may be a symptom of a nutritional deficiency, stress or parasites. You will notice feathers on the bottom of the cage and patches of feather loss on the bird itself. There should be no noticeable feather loss (bald patches) on the bird during a normal molt.

INTERNAL PARASITES

Coccidiosis is caused by a protozoan organism in a canary's intestine. The bird may show no symptoms, or it may have diarrhea. Other internal parasites include roundworms and tapeworms. Be sure to quarantine new birds and test for parasites if you house your birds outside.

MYCOPLASMA

This disease is associated with respiratory infection in canaries. Take your bird to a veterinarian if it exhibits respiratory symptoms.

SCALES

If your canary is allowed free flight in the house, be sure to keep a close eye on it.

Older canaries may develop scaly legs. Other scales are often due to a mite infestation and can be treated by a veterinarian. Be sure to look often at your bird's legs for any abnormalities.

What to Do if Your Canary Flies Away

It is not recommended to clip a companion canary's wings. If a cage is left open or a free-flying canary has access to an open door or window, it could take off into the outdoors. Oh no! If you are there, your initial reaction will probably be panic, but time is of the essence and your observation skills are needed.

Follow the canary with your eyes. Your best chance for getting it back are to know where it has gone. Some caged canaries will not have a great deal of endurance, and you will be able to catch them where they finally land, exhausted.

If you don't catch your canary right away, or it has landed at a distance or in a high tree, it at least helps to know where it is. Often canaries that are allowed free flight in a home return to their cage. They know that their cage is a familiar place where food and security are provided. If you know where your canary is, take its cage to that location in full view, with a fresh supply of its favorite seed or feed. If you aren't sure where your canary is, put its cage outside your house. Your canary hasn't been outside your house, so it won't know landmarks and figure out how to find its way home. Offering a familiar object outside is a good idea. Birds have sharp eyesight, and hopefully it is looking for its cage.

Another way to attract your canary is through vocalizations. Prepare for an emergency by making a recording of your canary's song, or by purchasing a canary song recording. Your canary probably has a preference for a certain genre of music or maybe even a favorite song. Be sure to have a recording of this when you go out. It will encourage your bird to sing back to you or to return to the sound of "home." Play your recording at frequent intervals to try to attract your bird back to your house and its cage.

If your canary flies away, try to follow it with your eyes and see the direction in which it went.

While you still have an idea where your canary headed on its flight outside, walk in that direction carrying your canary recording with you, or whistle your bird's favorite tune. Stop now and then to listen for a reply.

Sometimes it is helpful to know that birds cannot fly when wet. People who recapture lost birds use this knowledge to recover birds by drenching them with a hose then going up to pluck them off their perch. Also keep in mind that birds settle in to roost for the night. Double your efforts to find your bird in the evening, when it will be looking for a spot to spend the night.

Spreading the Word

If your initial efforts are to no avail, it's time to alert your community about your lost bird. Many papers run free "lost" ads in the classified section. You can search the Internet specifically for "lost bird" lists. Be sure to provide some clearly worded description about your bird's appearance. What color is it? Does it have distinctive markings, a crest or a recognizable song? Is it banded? On which foot? What color is the band? Don't forget to include your phone number and e-mail address.

To alert your neighborhood, make posters and get them out as quickly as possible. Post them at the grocery store, pet store, veterinary office and Laundromat, as well as throughout your neighborhood. Be as specific as possible. Write "LOST CANARY" in big letters. Describe your bird's color and any identifying markings. Use common language. If you have a variegated canary, don't say that. Say, "light yellow canary with black markings. Black spot over left eye and at base of tail," or something like that. The public isn't familiar with canary jargon, but conscientious animal owners will want to know if they're on the lookout for a yellow, white or apricot colored bird. List whether your canary has a band, the color of the band and what foot it is on. If you have a good photograph of your canary, include it. A picture is worth a thousand words in this case. If possible, make color posters or posters including a color photo. Canaries aren't the easiest birds to photograph; if you don't have a good close-up image of your own canary, perhaps you can photocopy one that resembles your bird from a book or magazine. Even if you haven't lost your canary, prepare for this emergency by being on the lookout for good quality photographs that

---

BE PREPARED

- Record your canary's song or buy a canary song recording.

- Record or purchase your bird's favorite music.

- Photograph your bird.

- Clip a photograph resembling your canary from a magazine or make a color photocopy of one from a book.

- Purchase or borrow a bird net and learn how to use it.

- Make color posters with a photo and a clear description of your lost canary.

---

resemble your bird. Also, take the opportunity to buy a canary recording, or at least be alert to your canary's favorite music. In your home, you have probably not needed a bird net to handle your canary, but you might want to have one on hand just in case your canary escapes. It would also be a good tool to reach your bird in a tall tree.

Continue alerting your community about your lost bird. Call the local animal shelter, your avian veterinarian, area veterinarians and pet stores. Call the local bird club and ask them to post a notice about your lost bird in their newsletter. A canary may be attracted to the seed at bird feeders, so it's probably wise to alert the local Audubon society or bird watchers as well. They will notice a new bird at their feeders, especially a canary.

What is the potential outcome for a canary that strays from home? It varies. Some companion birds are easy prey for cats, dogs and birds of prey. A canary that is used to human company may light on someone, perch on a house window or fly into a new home. Often, the general public considers this a windfall and doesn't look for a grieving owner. They have a new pet. This may be a happy outcome for the bird, if it receives adequate care, but it leaves the original owner grieving and worrying. A canary in good condition may join a flock of sparrows or finches and flit about your neighborhood for a while. If your bird is vividly

> ### COMMUNITY ALERT
>
> If your bird escapes, take the following measures:
>
> - Place a "lost "ad in the newspaper.
> - Hang posters in your neighborhood.
> - Contact the Humane Society.
> - Contact pet stores.
> - Contact veterinary offices.
> - Contact bird watchers.
> - Contact area bird clubs.
> - Search Internet lost-bird sites.
> - Browse Internet e-mail lists.
> - Contact friends with birds.

marked, being in a flock will provide some protection, but the canary will still stand out to a potential predator. Hopefully your communication with bird watchers will pay off!

You shouldn't underestimate how far a companion bird can fly. Your bird may be extremely frightened and take off for miles. Include a radius of 3 to 10 miles in your search and in your publicity efforts.

Finally, don't give up hope. Use all of your resources to find your bird. Follow up leads and connect with your pet-loving community. I wish you the best in your efforts if your bird flies away!

Preventing Canary Escape

You may never have to worry about finding a lost canary if you take precautions to make sure your canary does not escape. Obviously, you should be mindful of your canary's whereabouts when you open outside doors and windows. If you ever let your canary out of its cage for some flight time, be sure that all of the doors and windows are closed and that you expect them to stay that way.

Install screens on your windows. This protects your canary from mosquitoes, which are disease carriers, and keeps your bird inside. Check that all of your cage doors close securely, and make a habit of checking that you close the cage door after caring for your canary. Get in the habit of doing a double check.

If you have your birds in a screened porch or aviary, be sure to design it with a "safety" entrance. That is an entrance that leads into a small area where the door to the aviary is located. You can stand in the "safety" and close the door to the outside before opening the door to the bird's enclosure. This prevents losing birds that dart out when their owner comes into the aviary.

Band your canary so that you can identify it should it escape. You can choose a distinctive plastic band for your bird if it doesn't have one. If your canary has a

---

PET LOSS SUPPORT HOT LINES

University of California/Davis (Monday through Friday, 6:30 to 9:30 p.m. PST), (916) 752-4200

Companion Animal Association of Arizona (24 hours), (602) 995-5885

University of Florida, (904) 392-4700, ext. 4080

Tufts University Pet Loss Support Hot Line (508) 839-7966 (Tuesday and Thursday, 6:00 to 9:00 p.m. EST)

Delta Society Pet Grief Support Program in Seattle, Washington, (512) 227-4357

Grief Recovery Institute, (800) 445-4808

band already, write down the band's number, year and codes and put this information in a safe place should your bird ever get lost. Also make sure your canary's band number is part of your bird's veterinary records.

Finally, closely supervise the time your canary spends outside its cage. Don't take lightly your responsibility to watch over your feathered friend and its safety. And, oh yes, enjoy!

When Your Pet Canary Dies

When your pet canary dies, it is natural to grieve. You will miss your friend and companion, and may even feel some guilt about the loss of your canary. For your own peace of mind, it is usually helpful to bury your pet with some formality, and to take time to honor what it gave you during its life. If you would like support during your grief, there are several hot lines throughout the country with staff trained to work with you.

If you have several birds and your canary died suddenly, consider having your avian veterinarian do an autopsy. Wrap your canary's body in foil inside a plastic bag, and refrigerate it until you can have an autopsy done. You can't wait too long to arrange for this. You want to be sure that your canary did not die of a transmissible disease. If it did, you can treat the birds who are in your care and have been exposed.

Enjoying
Your

part three

Canary

chapter 8

Fun
with
Canaries

Canaries can be fun. It's not rough-and-tumble play like with a puppy, nor like the fun of having a parrot talk back to you. But canaries can be a delight to watch, and they are certainly a delight to the ear. Having a canary or becoming involved in breeding and showing canaries is a hobby that will immeasurably enrich your life. Owning a canary might lead to you becoming involved in a bird club. There are other people in bird clubs who are as charmed by their birds as you are by yours. They will lend an ear when you have stories to tell and may have some advice you could use, or may need some of yours. If you want to become even further involved with your hobby, you can consider going to a few bird shows and taking an interest in breeding and exhibiting birds.

Once you are filled with joy at owning a canary, the urge to share its song and its care can be overwhelming. It's possible to share by helping to place appropriate canaries in classrooms and senior centers in your area. Closer to home, more fun with your canaries may mean installing an indoor or outdoor aviary, allowing your canaries time outside in summer, or setting up a bird room at your house.

Bird clubs can be found in many communities throughout the country. I encourage you to start one if it turns out there isn't one close to you! Some bird clubs put on shows, others have members who are mostly pet owners. Still other clubs have a large percentage of bird breeders as members. They all have monthly meetings, educational speakers and special social events during the year. Most publish a monthly newsletter as well. You can go to socialize, though I encourage you to volunteer to get the most out of bird club membership. You can use your skills, meet new people and share your love of birds with others at a bird club. To find one, search on the Internet, ask at local pet stores and at your avian veterinarian's office and check in the back of national pet bird magazines. They often list clubs and events.

Waterslagger hen.

Photographing Your Canary

It's fun to share your canary with others. When you go to a bird club meeting or attend a seminar or even while you're waiting in a line somewhere, a photo is the easiest way to share. Canaries are small, active birds, which poses special problems for photographers. In first attempts at photographing a canary, the result is often a photograph featuring a little spec in the picture. The spec is bright yellow or orange, and you can point to it saying, "That's my canary, Fred!" Another common result, when you work at getting in close to the bird, is that the picture is all washed out, making it look like a ghost image of your canary. With

103

the most active birds, photos look like the tip of a wing or the end of a tail flying or hopping out of the picture. Though I can't guarantee a professional photo for you, I can help you make your photos better and give you some idea on how to take them.

First, you will have to consider equipment. With larger birds, most cameras are appropriate. For a canary, which is small, you need to be able to focus on the bird and fill up the frame with the subject. You will need a camera with a setting for close-ups, or a Single Lens Reflex (SLR) camera with interchangeable lenses. You can take canary photos either with a macro lens or a

wide-angle lens, both of which allow you to get close to your subject, or with a telephoto zoom lens, which allows you to be far away but to focus on a small subject.

With the macro lens or a wide-angle lens, you will need to filter the light from a flash

It is important to get up close when photographing your canary and to use a contrasting background.

because you will be close to the subject. Attach a white tissue over the camera's flash, but without covering the light sensing device on the flash unit. That will filter the light and allow your canary's colors to show. This is a process of trial and error, so be prepared to take a few rolls of film before you get it right! Another thing you can do is bounce the flash's light. Point your flash at a white wall or a white sheet and let the light bounce onto the subject of your photo. Requiring more equipment, you can also buy extensions for a flash that allow you to hold the flash away from the camera and the subject. Sometimes photographers need four hands to accomplish their task!

The best photos are not taken candidly, but are set up. You don't have to go out to a studio to set up a good photograph. All that matters is what's in front of the lens of the camera, and hopefully that's not the dirty dishes in the kitchen sink. You can use poster board, towels, art paper, burlap or a wall as a background. Blue or pastels work well for canaries and create less

contrast in your picture than either dark or light backgrounds. A natural branch is an artistic looking perch. Because canaries flit about and are rarely tame, you'll have the best success setting up a background in a cage (hopefully a fairly large one) and putting one perch in. Focus on a spot on the branch, and wait for the canary to land there. Have I mentioned yet that patience is an asset to bird photography?

Foliage makes a nice backdrop for a canary photo.

Having someone help you guide the canary to that spot is helpful. You can have a treat there, too, if you want to get an "action" shot and encourage the bird to stay in one spot for a while.

If you become proficient at setting up your shot, but want to start adjusting lighting, there are extra flash units that you can get to go off when your camera's flash goes off. You can use them to light up the background, eliminating some shadows, or to create studio effects with light from above a subject, or coming from one side. You may also need to diffuse the light from slave sensors if they are located close to your subject.

You can use foliage in the background of your photos for variety or for a nice effect. You'll have the fewest problems with shadows if you can locate your perch and bird at a distance from the background.

Try to get your canary to perch on a branch a couple feet in front of a backdrop, and use a telephoto lens and flash. The distance from the subject diffuses the light from my flash in this instance, and I am able to put up slave sensors at a distance also, so that they create more ambient light but not a burst of flash. You can try to do a similar setup in an aviary, or if your canary is especially tame, you may be able to work in your living room.

Try to recreate photographs you admire. The secret to successful photography is taking photos. Lots of photos. You'll get better if you analyze the ones you take, work out ways to improve them, and try again. Take your film to a photo lab to have it developed, and talk over the resulting photos with the staff. Chances are they will have some tips for you on ways to improve your photography.

The other secret to good photography, the hardest advice to take, is to discard the photos that are not your very best work. In a whole roll of film, often only one or two photos really turn out well. The rest go in the garbage. Fortunately, no one ever has to know about those.

BATHING SHOW BIRDS

Show birds are offered a bath each day or are sprayed by the bird breeder. They may use plain water or one of these mixtures:

2 tablespoons of mouthwash to 1 quart of water

1 tablespoon mouthwash plus 2 teaspoons glycerin to 1 quart of water

1 teaspoon each: mouthwash, Epsom salts, malt vinegar, glycerin to 1 quart of boiling water. Use this spray while it's somewhat hot.

Bird Shows

If you are intrigued by exhibiting canaries, it is wise to go to a bird show with several canary entries. Doing so is almost guaranteed to give you an urge to participate. You will probably see most of the kinds of canaries listed in this book, as well as beautiful specimens of many other kinds of finches and parrots. Birds you have never seen "in person" will be there. It's a great way to get to know what species look (and sound) like.

The best way to learn more about what is going on is to volunteer to be a "steward." These are the people who move cages for the judges. You'll learn how the birds are classified and what a judge is looking for in an exhibition canary. The basic reason for having shows is to let bird breeders show their best canaries in similar shape and color cages and to let an impartial, trained judge select the best birds.

Getting Ready for a Show

The show is the end result, but quite a bit has gone into preparing for it. About two months before the show, many exhibitors looked carefully at their canaries to determine which ones would do best at a show. They probably caught the bird, examined its feather quality, pulled bent feathers and checked for a full set of toenails. Of course, a missing toenail makes

no difference in the genetic quality of a canary for breeding, but it is a fault on the show bench. The chosen birds then live in separate cages until and during the show season. This way they cannot be picked on by other birds. This gives an exhibitor a chance to look closely at the chosen birds, as well. Do they carry themselves well, do their wings cross, are their chests and heads and carriage perfect? Usually a breeder will choose a male if he shows color-bred birds because they show the most vibrant coloring.

These birds are going to look their best, glossiest and sleekest. The birds can be brushed and combed with an eyebrow brush. Their nails should all be trimmed. For a few weeks before show season, in the interest of neatness and natural coloring, the canaries are not given greens.

A team of Waterslager canaries compete in a singing contest.

Show Cage Training

Training a canary to show well involves getting it used to a show cage and to people going by its cage. Many top exhibitors hook a show cage to the door of a canary's cage, until it starts hopping in and getting accustomed to the unfamiliar, small enclosure. The birds may be taken out in their show cage to different places, to get used to riding in the car and to seeing the different faces.

The prepared exhibitor packs a few essentials and some emergency supplies when heading off to a show. Bring along tissues, cotton swabs, black electrician's tape to close cage doors, a brush, scissors and a blood coagulant for emergencies. A magnifying glass and nail clippers are useful, too. These supplies are used to spruce up their show birds before judging, clean off the birds' vents and give the prized birds a last misting.

Getting to a show requires either a car ride or a plane trip. On a plane, the birds will usually ride with the exhibitor and their show cages are shipped to the hotel where the show is taking place. For more information on traveling with your pet bird, see "Traveling with a Canary," later in this chapter.

The Show

Shows happen in the fall in the U.S., starting in October and running through mid-December. The National Cage Bird Show, a goal for top-notch exhibitors, is held the third weekend in November. On Friday evening, the sponsoring bird club is busy setting up the room. There are tables for vendors, racks for the smaller birds, tables for larger birds. The judging area has a waist-high table and is fitted with full-spectrum lights so that the judge can see a bird's true colors, its best features and its faults. People from out

Prepare your bird well before show day so that it will perform at its peak (yellow variegated Consort Gloster).

of town will be arriving at area hotels, offering their canaries a last good bath, then bringing them in to register and spend the night in the show hall so they are familiar with their surroundings.

Each exhibitor pays a fee to enter each bird. The birds are shown in standard cages, which vary between the different breeds. They are painted a standard color inside, usually black outside, and there is at least ½ inch of seed in the bottom of the show cage. The cages are fitted with small waterers, which you will see nervous exhibitors attending to as they set up and between events.

The exhibitor gets a tag for each entry, on which he or she must write the correct breed and class for that canary. A show catalog lists all of the classes, and an exhibitor often gets one ahead of time. Classes are divided by sex and/or color of canary, and often by old or young (this year's babies). The tag is completed, including the exhibitor's name. That part of the tag is folded closed and stapled so that judging is anonymous. The exhibitor knows that to win he needs to be showing a banded canary he has bred himself. A lot of preparation has gone into this moment!

After birds are settled and the paperwork is completed, old friends join up for dinner or go home to dream of getting a prize the next day. A few more entrants arrive on Saturday morning, then the judging begins. Judges are usually flown in from throughout the country and have been trained and certified by the national specialty societies to judge the quality of the birds they specialize in. Usually they have been exemplary exhibitors of the types of birds they now judge. A few canaries at a time are presented to the judge, who starts placing them on the "bench" in the order he is ranking them. He sends some back, others come up. Good judges usually explain why they are choosing a certain bird. It is quite an educational experience to be present during judging. Is it its stance, coloring, size or similarity to the standard for that breed?

The best birds at the show know how to pose (variegated Corona Gloster)

FINAL SELECTION AT A SHOW

Birds are judged for a few seconds, at best a few minutes. They need to stand up straight and look their best at that time to win. The best birds seem to know they are gorgeous and pose beautifully. They have been carefully trained so that nothing at a show bothers them. Or at least they are veterans of shows and know what to expect!

Finally, the judge chooses the top ten birds in the class he is judging. The audience has had to stay quiet and be respectful, not letting on who bred which bird. When winners are chosen, they receive ribbons on their cages. Often, the top bird from this class will compete against the top birds in the other classes for a "best in show." When all the judging is over, tags are opened and you can see who bred the best birds.

On Saturday evening, winners are announced at a banquet and the exhibitors receive prizes and trophies for

Traveling with your canary can be fun, but make sure it's not fun for predators, too!

their winning birds. People visit, catch up on events over the past year and make new friends. This is a good time to ask lots of questions of people who know about breeding and exhibiting canaries. On Sunday, the show is often open to the public; there are sales tables at which you can buy a canary or canary supplies. There may be a raffle or auction as a fund-raiser.

There are both fulfilled and unfulfilled expectations among exhibitors. There are new champions. There are old friends and new ones. There may be some new breeding stock going home to the aviary, some babies sold. Usually a show weekend is full of highs and lows, always fun!

Traveling with a Canary

At some point you may wish to take a trip or you may plan a move that entails traveling with your canary. You can do it! First, decide how you two are going to travel. Do you want to travel by car, rail, bus or plane? Your real choice is car or plane. Your pet canary is not accepted by trains or buses.

CAR TRAVEL

Your canary can travel in the car in its own cage or any small cage that fits in your car. You should prepare the cage for travel. Any swings or hanging toys should be removed while the canary is in transit. Instead of water, which would slosh about during a drive, provide a juicy fruit or vegetable. Some leaf lettuce or an orange or slice of apple is appropriate. When you stop for a break yourself, offer your canary some water to drink and a chance to bathe. Since water quality varies across the country, bring some water from home or carry a brand of bottled water your canary is used to drinking.

Some canaries may be bothered by unaccustomed scenery whizzing by on a car ride. You can be prepared for this by carrying a cover for your bird's cage. A light colored sheet is perfect. It allows light in, but disguises the scenery.

Canaries are sensitive to extreme temperatures and to temperature changes. Remember this if you travel when the weather is hot or cold. Be sure to moderate the temperature in your car. If the weather is cold, protect your canary from the cold when transporting it to or from your car by covering the cage. In hot weather, carry a spray bottle filled with water. Giving your canary a misted bath will help keep it cool.

> ### CHECKLIST FOR CAR TRAVEL
>
> • Remove swinging objects from cage.
>
> • Carry a light cover.
>
> • Keep a water bottle handy.
>
> • Carry water from home.
>
> • Serve greens and fruit in water dish.
>
> • Protect your canary from heat and cold.
>
> • Be considerate at pet-friendly hotels.

As with any animal, don't leave a bird in an unattended car on a hot day. Watch your canary for its reaction to the temperature. If your canary is hot, it will hold its wings out from its side, sleek all its feathers down and open its beak, panting. If your canary is cold, it will fluff its feathers, trying to retain body heat, and may shiver.

If your car trip will take more than a day, you will have to think about accommodations. There are books available about hotels and motels that accept pets. You can search the Internet for pet-friendly hotels or inns on your route. Most Motel 6 units do accept pets, making your travels easier. Be sure to pick up after your pet, so that we all keep the right to travel with our

When your trip is through, make sure to put your canary in its regular cage as soon as possible.

animal companions. Put a towel or sheet under your bird's cage, clean up your messes and be considerate of the hotel and staff. You don't have to worry about noise when traveling with a canary. For one, birds are quiet at night, when fellow travelers might be disturbed. For another, canary song is quite pleasant!

When traveling by motor home or camping along your route, I can't think of anything more homey than a singing canary along on such adventures. Your canary will enjoy being outside on camping adventures, though you should be nearby to supervise its outside time. Even a caged canary is vulnerable to cats, raccoons or birds of prey and needs your protection. As always, protect your canary from high or low temperatures, direct sun and inclement weather.

PLANE TRAVEL

If you will be traveling by plane, you'll need to think ahead. Call your airline to see if a companion animal can travel with you. You will be able to make a reservation for your bird to fly with you in the cabin. The airline can advise you about an appropriate carrier for your bird and about state health regulations for your destination. Many states require a veterinarian's health certificate for animals traveling into that state. Your avian veterinarian will also be familiar with these regulations.

The Right Carrier

An appropriate carrier for birds that fly (by airplane) has sloped sides for adequate air ventilation. It should not be large, so that a bird could flail around and hurt itself. Rather it should be a cozy space with a perch and a bowl available. For airline travel, don't supply your canary with water, rather furnish it with leafy greens or

slices of apple or orange—juicy fruits and vegetables
that won't spill as water can. For cage flooring, consider putting in a substrate that affords good footing
for your canary. This might be a piece of Astroturf, or
paper towels.

If your canary does get detained in transit or separated
from you somehow, you will want to be located and you
will want whoever has your canary to be able to provide
for it. A bird's needs seem simple, but bird care is not
common knowledge! Be sure there are name and/or
address labels on your carrier, with phone numbers for
you at home and at your travel destination. In this new
information age, maybe you should include an e-mail
address. Also, tape care instructions
to the carrier. Include the need for
fresh water and new feed. Explain
that hulled seeds on the top of a
dish may make a dish appear full,
but are not edible. List a few of the
fresh treat foods your bird enjoys.
Maybe someone could get some
from an airport restaurant. You
hope these instructions are not
needed, but they would be invalu-
able in the event that you are separated from your pet bird.

Traveling Cargo

Here's an entirely different sce-
nario. If the airline on which you
are traveling does not allow companion animals in the passenger
area, or if someone else is taking an
animal on-board, and the airline
only allows one animal per trip, you
may consider shipping your canary
on the same plane, but in the cargo
hold. If you do so, be aware that
having a proper kennel and ade-
quate labeling is important. There are strict airline regulations about the temperature at which live animals

---

**CHECKLIST FOR
AIR TRAVEL**

- Make reservations for your
  bird. (If your bird is traveling
  in the cargo hold, check prob-
  able weather and schedule
  flights when the temperature is
  likely to be acceptable for animal travel.)

- Get a health certificate from
  an avian veterinarian if
  required (often within 10 days
  of the trip).

- Obtain a suitable kennel carrier and modify it for your
  bird. Include a perch, substrate with good footing and
  bowls.

- Put name labels and "up"
  notation on travel kennel.

- Supply greens and fruit
  instead of water.

- Attach care instructions and
  extra feed to kennel.

- Relax.

may be shipped. Ask your airline when you make reservations, as you may have to fly early in the day or overnight in order to meet requirements. Temperature requirements pertain to all airports on the trip, even if you are only planning a stopover somewhere.

You will probably be able to take your canary up to the front desk to check it in, and sometimes you are allowed to walk it down to your plane's cargo area. As for travel in the passenger area, label your canary's kennel appropriately, and include care instructions and extra feed taped to the outside. Mark which end is "up" for the smoothest ride for your little feathered friend! I have shipped birds on several occasions, and it has worked well for the bird. I was personally a nervous wreck, thinking of what turbulence, take off and landing must feel like to a bird who doesn't understand what's happening. Nevertheless, my birds have always arrived at their destination in a cheerful mood and have usually made friends along their journey.

**STOCKING YOUR
BIRD ROOM**

Your bird room could include any of the following:

- full-spectrum lighting
- tile or linoleum floor
- easily washable walls
- air purifier
- automatic feeders/waterers
- large flights for birds
- plants
- posters of birds on the wall
- access to a sink
- closet for storage

Building an Aviary or Bird Room

Fantasize a moment about what you would like to provide for your canary. Access to the sun? Room to fly? An environment filled with plants and branches and swings? Many people have turned a room in their house into a bird room, making that the pleasant, easy-to-clean habitat for their bird or birds. Then they decorate appropriately.

AVIARIES

Aviaries are outside, and may take some expertise to build. It's a good idea to visit several aviaries before building your own. By the time many bird lovers have built their second or third aviary, they usually incorporate additional features into it. No matter what the scope of your aviary, plan to incorporate a "safety" area you step into, with double doors to the outside and one to the aviary. You will not regret it. Losing a bird out a door is heartbreaking. Keep a few pointers in mind:

- Mouse-proof your aviary with cement, steel flashing or hardware cloth.

- Build your aviary close to the house so you can still go there in inclement weather.

- Offer your birds shelter on the side of the aviary that the wind comes from (often the north).

- Have both inside and outside quarters.

- Add both electricity and water to your aviary.

- If it gets chilly where you live, build removable shelter walls out of heavy plastic.

- If you are building in a basement, don't forget full-spectrum lights and a dehumidifier.

Canaries will love an outdoor aviary where they can fly freely and soak up some sun.

For inside flights:

- Consider adding casters to your aviary so you can move it to clean around it.

- Consider setting up a roll of paper so that it pulls under the flight and makes cleanup easier.

Sharing Canaries

Finally, your canary will be even more fun for you if you find a way to share it with others. Allowing a classroom to enjoy song for a few days, teaching neighborhood children about canary care or simply opening your windows in the summer or putting your canary on your porch or deck will be sharing! It's also possible that through your connections with a local bird club or through canary breeders you could help senior centers set up aviaries of their own. It would brighten up many sterile, petless facilities to do so. It has been proven that people live longer, are happier and recover faster from surgeries when they have pets in their lives. Canaries are so chipper and responsive, wouldn't that be an incredible gift to give?

chapter 9

Recommended Reading and Resources

Books

Walker, G. B. R. and Dennis Avon. *Coloured, Type & Song Canaries: A Complete Guide to Keeping, Breeding and Showing.* London: Blandford, 1993.

Harrison, Greg, Linda Harrison, Branson Ritchie, and Donald W. Zantop, eds. *Avian Medicine: Principles and Application.* Wingers Publishing, Inc., 1994.

Magazine Article

Parsons, James J., "A Detailed History of the Domesticated Canary." *American Cage-Bird* magazine, March 1989.

Internet Resources

The Connecticut Canary and Finch Club Home Page:
http://www.canaryfinch.com/ccfc/

American Singers Club, Inc.
http://www.upatsix.com/asc/

Southern Tasmanian Canary Society
http://www.tased.edu.au/tasonline/stcs/stcs.htm

Virginia Belmont's Famous Singing and Talking Birds
Canaries sing to classical music (on command)
http://www.petcraft.com/docs/vb.html

A Gallery of Canary Portraits
http://www.petcraft.com/docs/cangal.html

The Canary FAQ (Frequently Asked Questions)
http://www.upatsix.com/faq/canary.htm

The Link Between a Canary and King Tut
http://www.civilization.ca/membrs/civiliz/egypt/egt
ut04e.html

Northwest Roller Canary Club
http://www.wln.com/~desselle/roller.htm

Red Factor Canaries
http://www.redfactorcanary.com/

Join the Canary-L List:

To subscribe:

> In the body of the message: SUBSCRIBE CANARY-
> L yourfirstname yourlastname

To unsubscribe:

> In the body of the message: UNSUBSCRIBE
> CANARY-L yourfirstname yourlastname

LISTSERVE@idbsu.idbsu.edu

Images of the Canary Breeds:
http://www.alltel.net/~dorisann/can.html

Other Resources

AMERICAN SINGERS CLUB
2259 Charms Ravine Dr.
Wixom, MI 48393-4413

AMERICAN BORDER FANCY CANARY CLUB
348 Atlantic Ave.
East Rockaway, NY 11518

AMERICAN CANARY FANCIERS ASSOCIATION
13687 Camilla
Whittier, CA 90601

AMERICAN FEDERATION OF AVICULTURE
Box 52618
Phoenix, AZ 85079
(602) 484-0931

AMERICAN NORWICH SOCIETY
1604 NE 16th Place
Gainesville, FL 32609

AMERICAN SINGERS CLUB
4814 Liberty Ave.
Pittsburgh, PA 15224

AMERICAN WATERSLAGER SOCIETY
c/o Tom Trujillo, President
7918 Craddock Ave.
El Paso, TX 79915-4810
Phone: (915) 778-7015
Fax: (915) 496-2371
E-mail: trujillo@epenergy.com

AVICULTURE SOCIETY OF AMERICA
Box 5516
Riverside, CA 92517

BORDER CANARY ASSOCIATION (UK)
31 Abbotsford Rd.
Galashiels
United Kingdom

BRITISH ROLLER CANARY ASSOCIATION (UK)
18 Briary Ave.
High Green, Sheffield S30 4FY
United Kingdom

CANARY COLOUR BREEDERS ASSOCIATION (UK)
13 Gorse Crescent
Ditton, Maidstone, Kent
United Kingdom

CANARY COUNCIL FOR GREAT BRITAIN &
NORTHERN IRELAND (UK)
2 Belvedere Dr.
Wrexham, Clwydd WL1
United Kingdom

CENTRAL STATES ROLLER CANARY BREEDERS
305 Grosvenor Ct.
Bolingbrook, IL 60439

CONFEDERATION OF ALL CANARY TYPES
2801 Mayfield Dr.
Park Ridge, IL 60068

FIFE FANCY CANARY CLUB (UK)
6 Forbes St.
Alloa, Clackmannanshire FK10
United Kingdom

FRILL CANARY CLUB (UK)
396 Ashley Rd.
Poole, Dorset BH14 0AA
United Kingdom

GLOSTER BREEDERS ASSOCIATION (UK)
32 Bernwood Rd.
Headington, Oxford OX3 9LF
United Kingdom

GLOSTER FANCY CANARY CLUB (UK)
42 Teddington Gardens
Saintbridge, Glos
United Kingdom

INTERNATIONAL AMERICAN SINGERS CLUB
3584 Loon Lake Rd.
Wixom, MI 48096

INTERNATIONAL BORDER FANCY ASSOCIATION
1888 Mannering Rd.
Cleveland, OH 44112

INTERNATIONAL COLUMBAS FANCY
ASSOCIATION
305 Grosvenor Ct.
Bolingbrook, IL 60439

INTERNATIONAL FIFE FANCY CLUB OF AMERICA
11614 January Dr.
Austin, TX 78753

INTERNATIONAL GLOSTER BREEDERS
ASSOCIATION
1816 Trigg Rd.
Ferndale, WA 98248

LIZARD CANARY ASSOCIATION
Route 5
Paola, KS 66071

NATIONAL CAGE BIRD SHOW CLUB
25 Janss Rd.
Thousand Oaks, CA 91360

NATIONAL COLOR-BRED ASSOCIATION
236 Lester St.
Burleson, TX 76028

NATIONAL GLOSTER CLUB
58 Joanne Dr.
Hanson, MA 02341

NATIONAL INSTITUTE OF RED ORANGE
CANARIES
14 N. Wabash Ave.
Glenwood, IL 60425

NATIONAL NORWICH PLAINHEAD
CANARY CLUB
4347 W. Sandra Circle
Glendale, AZ 85308

NATIONAL ROLLER CANARY SOCIETY (UK)
51 Essington Rd.
New Invention, Willenhall, West Midlands
United Kingdom

NORTH AMERICAN BORDER CLUB
Route 3, Box 247
Jay, OK 74346

OAKLAND INTERNATIONAL ROLLER
CANARY CLUB
510 B St.
Santa Rosa, CA 95401

OLD VARIETIES CANARY ASSOCIATION
5513 Manor Rd.
Austin, TX 78723

SPANISH TIMBRADO
Alberto R. Berrios
Apartment 76
4204 Skipper Rd.
Tampa, FL 33613
(813) 979-4451

UNITED STATES ASSOCIATION OF ROLLER
CANARY CULTURALISTS
c/o Raul Thomas Sr.
533 Beach Ave.
Bronx, NY 10473

YORKSHIRE CANARY CLUB OF AMERICA
7616 Carson Ave.
Baltimore, MD 21224

For the latest information on shows, canary lists and
new sites, search for "canary bird" on the internet. If
you just search for "canary" you end up with the
Norwich, England, soccer team stats and sites having
to do with some specialized recording software!

If you have any questions or have a pet that you suspect
is experiencing problems call or visit the National
Animal Poison Control Center at http://www.napcc.
aspca.org/.

National Animal Poison Control Center
Suite 36
1717 S. Philo Rd.
Urbana, IL 61802
(800) 345-4735